SEA LIFE IN NELSON'S TIME

A TRUE BRITISH TAR.

SEA LIFE IN NELSON'S TIME

By

JOHN MASEFIELD

With an Introduction by Professor C.C. Lloyd

With Thirty-eight Illustrations

Third Edition

UNITED STATES NAVAL INSTITUTE

1971

© Conway Maritime Press Ltd.,
7 Nelson Road, Greenwich, London, S.E.10.

First Published 1905
Second Edition 1920
Third Edition — completely re-set
and with new illustrations 1971

In the United States of America
UNITED STATES NAVAL INSTITUTE
ISBN 0 87021 869 7

Library of Congress Catalog Card No. 77-175637

Set in 11/13 pt. Journal by P.J.B. Typesetting
& Printed in Great Britain by
Latimer Trend Ltd., Whitstable, Kent.

TO

CAPTAIN HENRY BAYNHAM, R.N.

ACKNOWLEDGEMENTS

The publishers wish to acknowledge with thanks the following:—

Miss D. Daniels for making available her considerable knowledge of Masefield and providing the source of the portrait of Masefield which appears on the jacket; Capt. A.J. Pack, R.N., of the Victory Museum, Portsmouth, for so willingly giving of his time; The Society for Nautical Research who administer the Victory Museum; the Naval Photographic Unit, H.M.S. Excellent, who provided a photographer and Wren assistant; Mr. & Mrs. A. Marr whose enthusiasm provided pleasant evenings on Ballast Quay.

John Masefield was unable to revise "Sea Life in Nelson's Time" as he wished to do, before he died, but it is felt that this new edition, with an introduction by Professor Lloyd and which has been completely reset and newly illustrated, goes some way towards achieving what Masefield would have wished.

The pictures were provided in the main by the Victory Museum, Portsmouth, with the following exceptions: plate 1, crown copyright, Science Museum, London; plate 6, Mr. & Mrs. A. Marr; plate 10, Greenwich Libraries; plate 14(b), H.M.S. Victory. The music was drawn by Peter Reeve.

CONTENTS

INTRODUCTION   xi

CHAPTER I

Page

Ship designing, building, sheathing, and rigging—The external decorations and appearance—The internal arrangements, deck by deck—The orlop and hold 1

CHAPTER II

The guns in use in our navy—Their nature—How loaded and fired—Varieties —Carronades—Shot—Small-arms—Gun-ports 14

CHAPTER III

The quarter-deck officers—The captain—The lieutenants—The master, second master, and master's mates—The midshipmen—The midshipman's berth 24

CHAPTER IV

The civilian and warrant or standing officers—The surgeon—The surgeon's assistants—The chaplain—The boatswain—The purser—The gunner—The carpenter—Mates and yeomen—The sailmaker—The ship's police—The ship's cook 39

CHAPTER V

The people—The boys—Manning—The divisions—The messes—The dress— The King's allowance—Grog—marines 54

CHAPTER VI

Sea punishments—The cat—Flogging at the gangway—Flogging through the fleet—Running the gauntlet—Keel-hauling—Hanging 71

CHAPTER VII

Page

In action 77

CHAPTER VIII

The daily routine—Sunday—Ship visiting 84

CHAPTER IX

In port—Jews—Lovely Nan—Mutinies—Their punishment—Sailor songs— "Drops of Brandy"—"Spanish Ladies," etc.—Flags—Salutes. . . . 91

EPILOGUE 100

BIBLIOGRAPHY 102

INDEX 104

LIST OF ILLUSTRATIONS

Frontispiece   A True British Tar

Facing page 20   Plate 1   Contemporary model of a 60 gun ship

Facing page 21   Plate 2   (a) Bar shot
                                    (b) Elongating shot
                                    (c) Shot carrier
                                    (d) Grape shot
                                    (e) Chain shot

Facing page 36   Plate 3   (a) A gun deck in action
                                    (b) The Marine stands guard

Facing page 37   Plate 4   (a) The Worm
                                    (b) The Sponge
                                    (c) The Powder Horn

Facing page 52   Plate 5   Cabin Boy to Admiral

Facing page 53   Plate 6   Poll of Plymouth's Prayer

Facing page 68   Plate 7   The Sailor's Prayer!!

Facing page 69   Plate 8   The Trafalgar Garter

Between pages 76 & 77 Plate 9   Knots of the period

    ”   ”   ”   ”   Plate 10   Nelson's funeral

    ”   ”   ”   ”   Plate 11   (a) Nelson Recreating with his Tars
                                    (b) Nelson aged 14
                                    (c) Brave Nelson's Last Lash

Facing page 84   Plate 12   The Veteran's address to a Young Sailor

Facing page 85   Plate 13   (a) Equity before Trafalgar
                                 (b) A mess-deck scene

Facing page 100   Plate 14   (a) John Bull taking a luncheon
                                 (b) Sailors in argument

Facing page 101   Plate 15   (a) Succefs to Nelson
                                 (b) A loving cup

INTRODUCTION

It is a pleasure to welcome a new edition of the clearest and most concise account of life at sea in Nelson's day, and for that matter in the days of a good many generations before him. Masefield's book was the first of its kind and though there have been many similar books since it was first published in 1905, it remains the most comprehensive introduction to the subject, even if it has long been out of print. It is not only a social study of the officers and men, how they were paid, fed and punished, but it also contains an excellent account of the technology of the period - the ships and guns and the way in which they were sailed and fought.

During the sixty years since it appeared a great number of contemporary journals have been published which give colour and depth to the picture. The late Michael Lewis and others have added the fruits of their researches, so that a generalisation such as the remark "It was reckoned that one-third of each ship's company was composed of lands-men, and that one-eighth of the entire number of men serving in His Majesty's ships were foreigners," needs a great deal of qualification as to the date of the type of ships before it is acceptable. Masefield used as his main sources the printed Admiralty Instructions and Regulations of the period, as well as the memoirs of officers, which were more widely read in those days than they are today. Occasionally, he quotes from a much earlier writer such as Edward Ward, but of contemporary reminiscences he only mentions Jack Nastyface and Samuel Leach, both of whom hated the navy. For the more technical aspects of his book, compilations such as *Falconer's Dictionary* and *Steel's Seamanship* served him well, as they were to serve C.S. Forester. Neither muster books nor any other manuscript material was used.

Perhaps the greatest virtue of the book, (which was more remarkable at the date it was written than it would be today), is the realistic picture it gives of the seaman's life. As he says, "Our naval glory was built up by the blood and agony of thousands of barbarously maltreated men." In the days of Jacky Fisher, this was not the angle from which naval history was usually approached.

For a writer on the age of sail, Masefield had the inestimable advantage of having himself served in windjammers round Cape Horn. At the age of thirteen he joined the *Conway* in 1891 and at fifteen he went to sea. The hardship of such a life impregnates much of his poetry, as well as the book. He soon gave up the sea as a profession and after trying a number of jobs in America he returned to London and became a freelance journalist. His first book of poems, published in 1902, contains the famous lyric *Sea Fever,* but he did not become well known as a poet until the publication of *The Everlasting Mercy* in 1911.

Sea Life in Nelson's Time was Masefield's first full length book. It was followed in 1906 by *On the Spanish Main* and *The Voyages of Captain William Dampier.* Then in 1907 came a study of Elizabethan life at sea in a long introduction to the six volume Everyman Library edition of *Hakluyt's Principal Navigations,* which is still valuable for the student of that period. For these books he read as widely as circumstances permitted. An old Conway shipmate once told him, "You were always reading, you were in your chest, or under a port, always reading." He himself wrote of his early years in London: "The years passed slowly, in continual toil of writing and much miscellaneous reading, chiefly historical. In this work I came to know how much of the past is buried in the British Museum and the Record Office and the methods by which some of it may be disinterred. I learned too, of the joy of research and some of the penalties of too much of it."
At the Museum he claimed to have once spoken briefly with Lenin: "Often I saw him walking slowly and sedately to some reference book-shelf. I saw that he was a visionary, always seeming to be looking at something very clear to him just above the level of his eyes, and to be smiling at what he saw, while nothing else much mattered.....Later I knew that this strange being was Lenin."

During the last half of his life he wrote an enormous number of books of poetry, drama romances and adventure stories. His poetry is not now in fashion, but as a prose author he is in the highest class as a writer of clear, muscular English, whether he is writing about the countryside which he loved so well, or, as in this book, the sea, with which he maintained that love-hate relationship which is the hallmark of the genuine seaman.

Christopher Lloyd, 1971.

Chapter I

Ship designing, building, sheathing, and rigging
The external decorations and appearance / The internal
arrangements, deck by deck / the orlop and hold

The ships in which Nelson went to sea were designed by master-shipwrights, in large sheds or studios known as "mould-lofts." There was a mould-loft in all the royal dockyards, near the dry docks or building slips. On the floor of a mould-loft the master-shipwrights drew the plans of their ships, at the full size of the intended vessel. On the walls, which were of great height, they chalked out their side elevations, from the keel to the prospective water-line, and from the water-line to the top of the poop-railings or hammock nettings, the parts farthest from the sea when the ship was afloat. Having chalked out their plans, and "laid down" their ships to their satisfaction, they gave orders for the timber to be cut in accordance with their designs. The work of building was then begun at that royal yard to which the mould-loft was attached. The chief yards were those at Chatham, Deptford, Plymouth, and Woolwich. The smaller ships were built on slips or launches, which sloped down to the water's edge. Large ships, or first-rates, designed to carry 100 guns, were generally built in dry dock, and floated out when completed by the admission of water.

The keel or backbone of the ship, the first wood to be placed in position, was "laid down" upon oak blocks distant some four or five feet from each other. The keel was generally of thick elm timbers, placed length-ways, which were "scarfed together," bolted and clinched at the sides. Under this keel, and to each side of it, in some ships, was placed a false keel of elm, lightly secured by copper staples. This false keel protected the main keel if the ship grounded. On this backbone or groundwork the hull of the ship was built.

Much of the oak used in the building of the ships was grown in England in the royal forests—such as the Forest of Dean in Gloucestershire, and the New Forest in Hampshire. The oak was very costly, for the service required the very best wood. It could not be, or should not have been, used for a year after cutting, for it needed to be seasoned before being handled by the shipwrights. On coming to the yards it was stacked for some months in sheds, in various positions, according to its future use, to allow it to season. Much of it was pickled, or boiled in a kiln for many hours, to allow the workmen to bend it to the frame of the ship. In times of stress much of it was used green—not properly seasoned.

The ships were built in the open air, and it was the custom to allow the frame or skeleton of every ship to stand exposed to all the airts "for a twelvemonth or a little more," before any timbers were placed across her ribs. It was thought that this exposure seasoned the oak of the frame. As a matter of fact, the constant wettings and warpings, from rain and sun, set up decay in the exposed wood, so that many ships had begun to rot "before a plank was put on." Some, indeed were as green as grass with mildew and fungus before the timbers were fitted. The general life of a ship in those days, built under these conditions, was only eight or nine years. Few lasted so long "without great repairs equal almost to their first cost." Many rotted to pieces after a few months at sea. In 1812 a fine three-decker, which had seen no hard sea service, was condemned as rotten a year after she was launched.

The timbers of these ships were secured to the uprights of the frames by long wooden pins, of oak or pitch-pine, known as tree-nails. The use of tree-nails was reckoned "a great cause of decay," but custom and thrift prescribed them. They were most insecure, as fastenings, for they were liable to shrink, so as to admit water to the middle of the plank. The plank when once wetted began to rot, and the shrunken tree-nail rotted with it, till at last the wooden bolt dropped from its hole, and the water obtained free admission. In those ships in which American oak had been used the decay set in more quickly than in other cases. These ships used to strain their seams or timbers open ever so slightly, in heavy weather, admitting water to the cracks. The wood so wetted began to develop dry-rot or fungus from the moment the water penetrated its fibres. Both fungus and dry-rot spread with strange rapidity when once it had established itself, and a ship so attacked had either to be pulled to pieces, so that the rotting oak could be removed, or broken up as useless.

To build a 74-gun ship, or third-rate (the most general rate employed in our navy), of about 1700 tons, nearly 2000 oak-trees were needed. Half of this number—perhaps a little more than half—were English grown. The other moiety was foreign oak, "very good for the ship bottoms, under water," but less lasting than the English kind. The foreign oak was sometimes American—and very subject to dry-rot—and sometimes from Silesia and Dantzic. An attempt was made to introduce cedar and scarlet logwood from Honduras, but the project failed, through the bankruptcy of the contractor. Fir was tried, at one time, for small ships of war, but it was too weak, and too little lasting, to be used for great ships. It was reckoned that a ship could be built for from £25 to £30 per ton, the actual cost of the oak being, on an average, about £7 per ton—a price much exceeded in the years subsequent to the death of Nelson.

When the ship was planked over and caulked she was sheathed below her water-line, to protect her timber from the teredo worm. Oak was very subject to the teredo, and many ships were practically eaten through, year after year, until 1758. In that year, a 32-gun frigate, H.M.S. *Alarm*, was sheathed with thin sheets of copper, against which the teredo worm was powerless. It was found that the copper also prevented the formation of barnacles and other filth which used to accumulate, many inches thick, on the bottoms of ships not coppered, impeding their way through the sea by several knots an hour. The first experiments with copper were not wholly satisfactory, for

2

the copper corroded the heads of all the iron bolts with which it came in contact. This was remedied to some extent by the use of a thin sheath of fir wood, which kept the copper from direct contact with the oak and the iron bolts. In 1783 iron bolts were abolished, and copper bolts, or bolts with copper heads, were substituted. After this, copper-sheathing became general throughout the navy and the merchant-service. The copper of condemned ships was stripped from the hulks at Portsmouth, and melted in a furnace, to clean it. It was then hammered out into sheets and used again. As a rule, brown paper was inserted between the oak of the ship's bottom and the sheets of copper.

Before the introduction of copper many experiments had been tried to keep out the teredo worm. Sheet-lead had been found too heavy, and not very efficacious. A layer of pitch, covered with successive layers of brown paper, tar, short hair, and thin deal plank, had been found effectual, if costly. A thin sheath of deal over the oak was better than nothing, for it took the worms some little while to get through to the oak, as they cared less for deal than for any other wood they attacked. A packing of lime, or a thorough washing with lime, was found to keep them away. There were also preparations of tar and tallow, and arrangements of hides and chemicals, which had their merits and demerits. Copper replaced all of these, though there was some little grumbling at the cost at the time of its first introduction.

As soon as a ship was built, sheathed, and launched, she was brought alongside a sheer-hulk, an old man-of-war cut down to her lower gun-deck. A sheer-hulk was fitted with a single mast in midships, to which was attached "an apparatus consisting of sheers, tackles, etc., to heave out or in the lower masts of His Majesty's ships." The "Establishment," or Admiralty scale, gave minute instructions as to the length and size of every spar to be supplied to each rate. A stock of masts was kept at each dockyard in a vat of pickle known as a mast-pond. For great ships, and indeed for nearly all the rates in the navy, the lower masts were "built," or "made," of two or more pieces of fir strongly hooped together with iron hoops. When a ship came alongside a sheer-hulk her lower masts and bowsprit were hoisted into her and stepped. The fore-mast was stepped at a distance of one-ninth the length of the lower gun-deck from the stem of the ship. The main-mast was stepped in the centre of the ship, or a little abaft the centre. The mizzen-mast was distant from the bow about seventeen-twentieths of the length of the lower gun-deck. The heels of all three masts were stepped or fixed in strong wooden sockets, or mortises, known as tenons, at the bottom of the ship's hold. These mortises or tenons were of oak, and the timbers which formed them lay across the keelson, or inner part of the keel. The bowsprit "steeved" or raked upwards at an angle of about thirty-six degrees with the horizon. The masts, as a rule, raked or inclined slightly aft, but the rake of a ship's mast was sometimes altered to suit her sailing. Some ships sailed better with their masts stayed forward, or stayed plumb, without rake.

When the lower masts and bowsprit were stepped and secured the ship received her rigging from the rigging-loft. Her lower rigging was then set up by master-riggers, helped by the marines and standing officers. The shrouds and stays which secured the masts were made of hempen rope, "three-strand shroud laid," tarred on the outside, but not within the lay of the rope. Wire rope, which is now used for nearly all standing rigging, was then unknown. When the lower rigging was all set up, and the rigging of the bowsprit finished, the jibboom and top-masts were sent aloft and rigged. When these were finished the flying jibboom and topgallant and royal masts were sent up and rigged, after which the ship's standing rigging was complete. The stays, the strong ropes which supported the masts forward, were always doubled.

When the standing rigging was complete, the yards, on which the square-sails set, were crossed on their respective masts. The yards were of fir, the lower yards being "made," or built, of more than one piece of timber. The upper yards were fashioned from single trees. Some captains of Nelson's time slung their lower yards with chain, a custom which in time became general. As a rule, however, the lower yards were slung with stout rope. The rig was practically that in use at the time of the abolition of sailing ships in the Royal Navy in the early sixties. There were, however, various differences. The sprit-sail, a square-sail on the bowsprit, setting from a yard underneath that spar, was still in use. The sail was not abolished until about 1810, while the yard, or a relic of it, remained for many years later, though no sail was set upon it. On the mizzen-mast the spanker or driver was not set upon a gaff and boom, but on a great lateen yard, pointing fore and aft, its lower and forward arm reaching down to a little above the wheel. Ships with these lateen "cross-jacks" were to be seen almost at the end of the eighteenth century. No ships carried sails above their royals, the fourth square-sail from the deck. Stay-sails were set between the masts, and studding-sails at the extremities of the yards. Perhaps the last change in rigging which Nelson saw was the introduction of the flying jib, and its boom, at the extremity of the bowsprit.

Masts, spars, sails, and rigging for ships of every rate were always kept in stock at the royal yards. The ships of the navy were built according to the "Establishment," or Admiralty regulations, each ship of each rate being as like as possible, so that the gear of one 74 would fit every 74 in the service. The theory was excellent, but in practice it failed, because many of the ships in our navy in Nelson's time were not built according to the "Establishment" but were captured from the French and Spanish. Indeed, the only good ships in our fleets were built by French and Spanish hands. The French treated shipbuilding as an imaginative art. The very finest brains in the kingdom were exercised in the planning and creation of ships of beautiful model. Admirable workmen, and the best talents of France, produced, in the latter half of the eighteenth century, a number of sailing men-of-war which were more beautifully proportioned, faster on every point of sailing, stronger, and with larger batteries, than the ships built in this country at that time. A French 80-gun ship at the close of the eighteenth century was bigger, more roomy, faster, and a finer ship in every way, than our 98-gun ships. Our own men-of-war were so badly designed and proportioned that they were said to have been built by the mile, and cut off as required. They were very cramped between-decks, yet they were nearly always pierced for more guns than they could conveniently fight. They were very crank ships, and so "weak" that they could not fight their lower-deck guns, in anything like weather. They were slow at all points of sailing, and slack in stays. In heavy weather they sometimes rolled their masts out, or sprung them by violent pitching. Had the French been able to improve their guns as they improved their ships our navy would have been destroyed. As it was, their superior sailing was to some extent neutralised by the fact that decisive naval engagements had to be fought at close range, within, say, a quarter of a mile of the enemy. The Spanish ships were but a little inferior to the French. A queer Irish genius named Mullins, who had settled in Spain, was the master-shipwright responsible for them. They were used (as some of our French prizes were used) as models by our English designers, but the English ships were not markedly improved till after the death of Nelson. The following table may help the readers to an understanding of the different rates in use. The figures are approximate.

	No. of Guns	Weight of Broadsides	No. of Men	Tonnage	Length of Lower Gun Deck	Cost (without Guns)
				From		
First-Rate	100, or more	2500-2550 lbs.	850-950	2600-2000 tons	180 ft.	£100,000-70,000
Second-Rate	98 or 90	2050-2300 lbs.	750	2000 tons	180-170 ft.	£60,000
Third-Rate	80, 74, or 64	1970, 1764 or 1200 lbs.	720, 640, 490	2000-1700,1300 tons	170-160 ft.	£54,000-36,000
Fourth-Rate	50	800 lbs.	350	1100 tons	150 ft.	£26,000
Fifth-Rate	44, 40, 38, 36, or 32	636-350 lbs	320, 300, 250, 215	900-700 tons	150-130 ft.	£21,500-15,000
Sixth-Rate	28, 24, 20	250-180 lbs.	200-160	650-550 tons	130-120 ft.	£13,000-10,000

Beside these there were many small, unrated ships, such as gun-brigs, sloops, ketches, schooners, cutters, etc., and some foreign prizes so armed that they could not be rated by the English scale. It must be noted that our official rating reckoned only the regular armament—i.e. the guns of the regulation patterns. After 1779 our ships carried carronades in addition to their other guns, but these were never reckoned in the Admiralty ratings.

Viewed from without, a first, second, or third-rate wooden man-of-war appeared ponderous and cumbersome. A modern sailor, accustomed to the keen iron-ships of the present day, would have called such a ship a sea-waggon, qualified or otherwise, before spitting and passing by. But when the great sails were set, and the hull began to move through the sea, the cumbrous hulk took on attributes of beauty and nobility. There has been, perhaps, no such beautiful thing on earth, the work of man's hands, as an old 74 under sail.

If one had taken a boat and rowed out to such a ship as she lay at anchor, fitted for the sea, towards the end of the eighteenth century, one would have been struck, first of all, by her bulk. The ships had bulging wooden sides, vast stern-works, and cumbrous wooden beak-heads. They set one wondering how oak of such thickness could have been wrought to such curves. Till Nelson's time there was no uniformity in the painting of the exteriors of the ships. The captains used their own discretion, and followed their own tastes, in the selection and application of the colours. The most general colour-scheme was as follows:—Along the water-line, just above the ruddy gleam of the copper-sheathing, was a wide black streak, running right round the ship, and reaching as high as the level of the lower gun-deck. Above this the sides were yellow, of a yellow sometimes inclining to brown, like the colour of certain varnishes, and sometimes of a brighter tint, like the colour of lemon peel. The after upper-works above the gun-decks, and the outer sides of the poops above the quarter-deck guns, were painted a vivid red or blue. This band of bright colour gradually faded, till by the time of Trafalgar it had become a very deep and dull blue, of a dingy tint that was very nearly black. A band of scarlet or pale blue, edged with gold, ran round the forecastle, and continued down the beak to the figurehead. The outsides of the port-lids were of the same colour as the sides—that is, of a brownish yellow. The stern-works were generally elaborate with gilded carving, gilt cherubs, and the like, and with red, blue, green and gold devices, such as cornucopias, drums and banners, royal arms, wreaths, etc. Round the stern of each ship, outside the glazed cabin windows (we are talking of a third-rate or 74-gun ship), ran a quarter gallery or stern walk, on which the captain could take his pleasure. The supports and rails of this walk were heavy with gold-leaf. First and second-rate ships had three and two stern walks respectively. At the bows, at the extremity of the great beakhead, was the ship's figurehead, either a ramping red lion or a plain white bust, or a shield, or some allegorical figure suggested by the name of the ship. The allegorical figure was, perhaps, the most popular among the sailors. They took great pride in keeping it in good repair, with bright gilt on its spear or helmet, red paint upon its cheeks, and pretty blue sashes wherever such appeared necessary.

The ships of Lord Howe's fleet, in 1794, appear to have been painted (externally) as follows:—The side of the ships above the line of the copper a dull brown tint; the tiers of ports a pale lemon yellow, chequered by the port-lids, the outsides of which were brown, like the sides of the ship. The gilded scroll-work, at bow and stern, was as usual. Lord Nelson is said to have painted the ships of his fleet after much the same pattern, only substituting black for the dull brown of the sides and outer port-lids. The arrangement used by him became popular. It was known as the "Nelson chequer": black sides and port-lids, and yellow streaks to mark each deck of guns. It was at first used only by those ships which had fought at Trafalgar or the Nile. In time it became the system adopted throughout the Navy. The captains of some ships preferred their own colour-schemes, and painted their vessels with red or orange streaks to mark the gun tiers. The "Nelson chequer" was, however, to become the colour arrangement generally

6

employed. Some years after Trafalgar the lemon-yellow ribands gave place to white, which continued in use till wooden men-of-war became obsolete. Those which remain afloat are painted black and white in the manner in use in the early sixties, when such ships ceased to be built.

Internally, the sides of the ships were painted blood-red, in order that the blood, which so often and so liberally spattered them, might not appear. The inner sides of the port-lids were painted of this colour, so that when the port-lids were opened, the brown or black of the ship's sides was diversified agreeably with scarlet squares. After Trafalgar the interiors of the ships of war were sometimes painted in other colours, according to the whims of their commanders. Green was the most common variant, but the interior of some ships was painted yellow or brown. A favourite arrangement was the white and green—white for the ship's sides and beams, and green for the waterways and coamings. White became the rule about the year 1840: Many internal fittings, such as gun-carriages, and, in some cases, the guns themselves, were painted red or chocolate. Lower masts were sometimes painted a dull brownish yellow. Top-masts and upper spars were covered with a dark brown preserving varnish. Yards and gaffs were painted black. Blocks, chains, dead-eyes, and wooden and iron fittings for the rigging, were tarred black to match the yards. The projecting platforms known as the chains or channels at the side of the ships, to which the lower rigging was secured, were painted to match the sides of the ships. As the masts of French ships were generally painted black, the ships in our fleets painted their masts white before any general engagement, so that the ships might be distinguished in the smoke and confusion.

The visitor going aboard one of these ships, and entering her, not by the entry port to the main-deck, with its little brass rail and carved porch, but by the gangway to the upper-deck, would have climbed from his boat by a ladder of battens nailed to the timbers. At each side of this ladder was a side rope, extended by iron stanchions. The rope, as a rule, was a piece of ordinary 3-inch hemp, worn smooth and shiny by many hands. For important visitors, such as a captain or flag-officer, special side ropes were rove, either of white cord or of the ordinary rope covered with green or scarlet cloth. Both the gangway and the entry port were guarded by a marine sentry, in a red coat, pipeclayed belts, and white knee-breeches. A midshipman kept watch about the gangway to report to the lieutenant the arrival of all boats coming to the ship before they drew alongside.

On gaining the deck of an old 74 the visitor would have found himself upon the spar-deck, just abaft the main-mast, fronting the great timber bitts, with their coils of running rigging. Close beside him was the quarter-deck ladder, leading up to the quarter-deck.[1] Above this again was the poop, a second raised platform or deck, reached by short, small ladders from the quarter-deck. Right at the stern of the ship, inclining outboard over the sea, was a flagstaff on which flew an ensign as large as a mizzen-topgallant-sail. If the visitor had clambered up the sloping deck to this point he would

---

1   *The quarter-decks of many ships were raised above the upper deck. In small ships of war, such as frigates, the quarter-deck was the after part of the upper-deck, below the break of the poop.*

have been able to overlook the whole of the upper surface of the ship. Just beneath him, at his back, below the step of the flagstaff, he would have seen a heavy lantern, or stern light, with a ponderous and decorated case. To each side of the flagstaff were lifebuoys, by which a marine with a hatchet was always stationed when the ship was at sea. At the alarm of "man overboard" the marine hacked through the lanyard supporting one of the lifebuoys and let it drop into the water. At each side of the ship, along the poop and quarter-deck, were the after-guns, which, till 1779, when the carronade was adopted, were generally 9-pounders, in red wooden trucks or carriages, secured to the ship's side in the usual way. These guns pointed through square port-holes which were cut, without lids, through the thick wooden bulwarks. Forward of the mizzen-mast, under the break of the poop,[1] or, in the later times, on the quarter-deck itself, was the great double steering wheel, placed in midships, abaft the binnacle which held the compass. The tiller ropes were made of raw-hide thongs, raw-hide being tougher than rope, and less dangerous to the crew when struck by a shot than chain would have been. Over the wheel hung the forward arm of the great lateen mizzen-yard,[2] a relic of Drake's time, which was not abolished in favour of the spanker gaff and boom until the end of the eighteenth century. Along the sides of the quarter-deck, and along the ship's bulwarks as far forward as the beakhead, were the hammock nettings, or hammock cloths, within which the hammocks of the ship's company were stowed.

Forward of the quarter-deck, between that deck and the forecastle, was the waist, or, as a modern sailor would call it, the well. It was not decked over, nor were the wooden bulwarks of the quarter-deck continued along it, but to each side, in the place of bulwarks, were iron standards, supporting two thick canvas breastworks or stout nettings of rope about two feet apart, between which the hammocks of the crew were stowed. Directly within these breastworks were broad plank gangways, for the convenience of the sail-trimmers, small-arm parties, and marines. Between the main and fore masts, in midships, parallel with the decked-over gangways, were the booms, or spare spars, tightly lashed in position. On the top of these spars, or to each side of them, were the ship's boats, long-boat, barge and cutter, with their oars and sails inside them. Farther forward was the forecastle, upon which were more carronades, or 9-pounder cannon, and one or two heavy bow-chasers, or guns made to fire forward. On the forecastle was the great ship's bell, hanging from a heavy wooden or iron belfry, with a plaited lanyard on the clapper to help the timekeeper to strike it. In the centre of the forecastle was the galley-funnel, the chimney of the ship's kitchen. At the forward end were ladders leading into the beakhead, from which the sailors reached the bowsprit when occasion sent them thither.

Under the poop was the captain's cabin, extending from its forward limit to the gilded stern gallery. This part of the ship, extending outboard as it did, like a great gilt excrescence, was sometimes known as the coach or round house. Very frequently this cabin contained no guns. If it contained guns they were seldom or never fired. The

1 *Or under the break of the quarter-deck.*
2 *Or "cross-jack"*

8

ports of the cabin were glazed, and there was a couch or settee running under them for the ease of the captain. These settees were hollow, and formed convenient cupboards for the captain's gear. As the floor or deck of the cabin was laid upon the beams of the main or upper gun-deck, it followed that the cabin was loftier and roomier than any other place in the ship. The poop, the deck above it, was raised some feet above the quarter-deck, as we have seen, so that the captain's state apartment may have been some eight or nine feet high. A door from it opened into the stern walk, which opened by two little doors, one on each side, to the quarter galleries. The cabins were usually very bare. They were furnished with a large fixed table, a few heavy chairs, a fixed or swinging sleeping cot, and a wooden washhand stand containing a basin. It was shut off from the forward portion of the ship by a simple wooden bulkhead, made of elm, so fitted that it could be lifted from its place and shifted out of its way when the ship went into action. In early times, in the days of the Stuarts, this bulkhead and the interior of the cabin were made gay with carved work, or, as it was then called "gingerbread work." Great ships of the first and second rates then carried joiners, to repair and keep beautiful these decorations. In the latter half of the eighteenth century the cabins were without decorations of any kind. The only breaks to the bareness of the wood were the captain's foul-weather clothes, dangling from pegs, and his lamp swinging in its gimbals or hinges, his telescope in his bracket, and, perhaps, a trophy of swords and pistols, or a stand of the ship's arms, such as muskets and cutlasses, in a rack about the mizzen-mast. There were, of course, captains like Captain Whiffle in the novel, or the scented Captain Mizen in the play, who lived in great splendour, in carpeted cabins hung with Italian pictures. These worthies kept perfumes burning in silver censers to destroy the odour of the bilge. Such captains were, however, the exception, not the rule. A captain with a case of books and a pair of curtains to his windows was regarded as a sybarite. Any decorations beyond these were looked upon as Persian and soul-destroying.

The forward bulkhead of the cabin was pierced with a door in midships, which opened on to the half-deck, the space covered by the quarter-deck. The half-deck was also known as the steerage, from the fact that the steering wheels and binnacle were placed there, under the roof or shelter of the quarter-deck planks. The sides of the half-deck were pierced for guns, generally carronades. It must be remembered that the half-deck was, as its name implies, decked over, so that one could walk from side to side of the ship on a floor of planks. The waist, or space between the fore and main-masts, on the same plane, was not so decked. The forecastle was decked across, and the sides of the forecastle were pierced for carronades. But there were no guns on the plank gangways along the sides of the waist, partly because the position was exposed, and partly because the space was needed in action by the sail-trimmers and small-arm parties. The raised forecastle and high poop and quarter-deck, were survivals from old time. In the old ships of war, of the reign of Elizabeth, these superstructures had been built of great strength and height, "the more for their majesty to astonish the enemy." No ship could be carried by boarding until the men defending these castles had been overcome. No boarding party could enter such a ship without great danger, for the bulkheads of these castles were pierced for quick-firing guns, mounted so as to sweep the waist. Any troop of boarders clambering into the waist could be shot down by the gunners in the castles. The superstructures were excellent inventions for that time, when naval engagements were decided by hand-to-hand fighting, or by ramming. They were less useful when the improvements in ordnance made it possible to decide a sea-fight by the firing of guns at a distance. They lingered in our Navy until the third or fourth decade of the nineteenth century, when the raised or topgallant forecastle was abolished. Some twenty or thirty years before this happened the quarter-deck and poop were merged together, so that there was then but one deck above the spar-deck.

Passing forward from the steerage one came to the main hatchway in the open space of the waist, just forward of the main-mast. The ladders of this hatch-way led from the waist to the deck below. This deck below the spar-deck was known in first and second rates as the main-deck. In third-rates, such as a 74-gun ship, it was called the second or upper deck. Right aft, on this deck, was the ward-room or officers' mess, where the lieutenants had their meals. The room was large and well-lit, for the stern of the ship was pierced with five or six windows, which were all glazed, like the windows of the captain's cabin. Part of the ward-room was used as an officers store-room, and this part seems to have been shut away from the rest by means of wooden bulkheads, made of elm, as being less liable to splinter if struck by a shot than any other sort of wood. There was no stern walk outside the after windows on this deck, but there were quarter galleries to each side. These were generally fitted up as lavatories for the lieutenants. Forward of the ward-room, on each side of the deck, were the state-rooms of the lieutenants—little fenced-off cupboards, walled with elm wood, each of them just large enough to hold a cot, a writing-desk, a chest of clothes, and a few instruments. In some ships—as in fifth and sixth rates—the lieutenants slung their hammocks in the ward-room, there being no space for private cabins. Beyond the ward-room bulkhead was the open deck, clear of obstruction save for the capstans and the openings of the hatchways, almost as far forward as the fore-mast.[1] Abaft the fore-mast, in midships, was the cook-room or galley, where the cook perspired over his coppers. The galley floor was paved with brick, to lessen the risk of fire. At each side of the deck, at their respective port-holes, were the lines of cannon. The general calibre for this deck, aboard a 74, was the 24-pounder. Of these there were usually some fifteen or sixteen at each side of the ship on this, the second or upper deck.

As a large portion of this deck was not decked over, but open to the sky, save for the boats and spare spars, the fighting space was comparatively light. In fine weather, and in moderately breezy weather, the gun ports on this tier could be kept open, at anyrate to lee-ward. In bad weather, when they were closed, when tarpaulins covered

---

1   *In some ships the space under the booms on this deck was fitted with a cattle-pen, in which the officers kept their live stock, if they had any. In fine weather, the deck about the cattle-pen was used by the various craftsmen of the ship. The armourer and blacksmith worked at their anvils about the galley. The carpenters sawed and planed at their tables. The sailmakers spread their canvas, and stitched, and put in patches. In fine weather the sick were placed here for the benefit of the air and the sun.*

the hatchways and open spaces, the deck was lit by the bull's-eyes—the round and oval plates of thick glass, which were let into the centre of the port-lids. At night the only lights allowed were cased in the battle-lanterns of thick horn. If the ship went into action at night the sailors fought their guns by the light these lanterns afforded, one lantern being placed beside each gun.

Beneath the second or upper deck was the first or lower gun-deck, the principal deck of the ship. It was the broadest of the decks, and by far the strongest, and the most roomy. Here the heaviest cannon, the two long batteries of 32-pounder guns, were mounted; and here, in action, was the fiercest of the fighting. Right aft, on this deck, was the gun-room, in which the gunner and his mess lived. It was also the ship's armoury, where the muskets, cutlasses and pistols were stored. The younger midshipmen sometimes slung their hammocks in the gun-room,[1] under the fatherly eye of the gunner. In some ships the gunner acted as caterer to the youngest of the midshipmen, and saw to it that their clothes were duly washed during the cruise. Forward of the gun-room bulkhead (or of the stand of arms mentioned below) there was the open deck, with the lines of guns in their blood-red carriages. The heavy rope cables stretched along this deck, in midships, nearly as far aft as the main-mast. Right forward, in midships, stretching across the bows, was the manger, a sort of pen, some four feet high, over which the cables passed to the hawse-holes. The manger was designed as a breakwater to keep the water which splashed through the hawse-holes from pouring aft along the deck. The hawse-holes were firmly plugged with oakum and wooden shutters when the ship was at sea, but no contrivance that could be devised would keep the water from coming in in heavy weather. The manger also served as a sheep-pen or pigsty or cattle byre, if the ship carried live stock. This lower-deck was the berth or sleeping deck, where the men slung their hammocks at night. It was also the mess-deck, where they ate their meals. The place was very dark and noisome in foul weather, for a very moderate sea made it necessary to close the port-lids, so that, at times, the crew messed in semi-darkness for days together. It was also very wet on that deck in bad weather, for no matter how tightly the ports were closed, and no matter how much oakum was driven all round the edges of their lids, a certain amount of water would leak through, and accumulate, and slop about as the ship rolled, to the discomfort of all hands. In hot climates the discomfort was aggravated by the opening of the seams of the deck above, so that any water coming on to that deck would drip down upon the deck below. Often in its passage it dripped into the sailors' hammocks, and added yet another misery to their miserable lives. In midships on this deck, round the hatchway coamings,[2] were shot racks, containing 32-lb round shot for the heavy batteries. The pump-dale, or pipe for conveying the water pumped from the hold, ran across the deck

---

1 *The youngest midshipmen sometimes slung their hammocks just outside the gunroom, in a space cut off from the rest of the lower deck by a stand of muskets and cutlasses extending across the deck. A marine stood guard at the entrance to the railed-off portion. He was generally a recruit, good for nothing else. He seems to have beguiled his hours of sentry-go by blacking the boots of the ward-room officers. Vide The Navy at Home.*

2 *Coamings are raised ridges round the hatchway openings, designed to keep the water from falling below in any quantity during foul weather. They also prevent the unwary from falling down the ladders.*

to the ship's side from "the well" by the main-mast. This was the sole obstruction to the run of the deck, from the gun-room to the manger, between the midship stanchions and the guns. There was a clear passage fore and aft, for the lieutenants in command of the batteries. In midships were the hatch-coamings, the capstans, the bitts and cables, and the stanchions supporting the beams. Between these obstructions and the breaches of the guns was a fairly spacious gangway, along which the officers could pass to control the fire.

Below the lower or first deck was a sort of "temporary deck," not wholly planked over, called the orlop or overlap-deck. It was practically below the water-line when the ship's guns and stores were aboard. It was therefore very dark and gloomy, being only lit by a few small scuttles, in the ship's sides, and by lanterns and candles (or "purser's glims") in tin sconces. Right aft on this deck was the after cockpit, where the senior midshipmen, master's mates, and surgeon's mates, were berthed. This cockpit was of considerable size, for here, after an action, the wounded were brought, to suffer amputation and to have their wounds dressed. The mess table, at which the reefers and mates made merry, was fixed in the middle of the berth. After an action it was used as an operation table by the surgeons. Adjoining the after cockpit were cabins for the junior lieutenants; state-rooms for the surgeon, purser, and captain's steward; the ship's dispensary; a little cupboard for bottles and splints, and the purser's store-room. In small ships of the fifth and sixth rates the marines berthed on this deck, abreast of the main-mast, hanging the beams with their pipeclayed belts and cartridge boxes. The spirit-room, about which the imaginative writer has written so imaginatively, was sometimes placed on this deck, near the after cockpit. More generally it was below, in the after hold.

Further forward, on the orlop-deck, the line of battleships had racks for the bags of the men and the chests of the marines, to which access could be had at stated times. In midships was the sail-room, or sail-locker, where the spare suits of sails were stowed. Here, also, were the cable-tiers, or dark, capacious racks, in which the cables were coiled, by candlelight, when the ship weighed her anchor. It was the duty of the midshipmen to hold the candles while this stowing of the cables was performed by the quartermasters. After a battle, when the after cockpit was filled with wounded men, the midshipmen and mates slung their hammocks in the cable tiers. To the sides of the cable tiers were other tiers for the stowage of spare rigging and hawsers. Beyond these again, stretching across the deck, was the fore cockpit, where the boatswain and carpenter had their cabins and store-rooms. The carpenter's store-room was filled with tools, and with the implements for stopping shot holes. Most of the actual carpentering was done above, in daylight, on the upper-deck. The boatswain's store-room contained blocks, fids, marline-spikes, rope yarn, etc., for the fitting and repairing of the rigging. In peace time, for some reason, the boatswain and carpenter slept on the lower-deck in cots or double hammocks slung in the most favoured places. In war time they kept their cabins.

Near the two cockpits were the entrances to the fore and after powder magazines, where the ship's ammunition lay. The hatches leading to the magazines were covered over by copper lids, secured by strong iron bars and padlocks. The magazines were only opened on very special occasions by the captain's order. A marine sentry stood at the hatch of each magazine with a loaded musket, to prevent any unauthorised person from tampering with the padlocks or trying to enter. In battle this sentry was reinforced by a corporal's guard with fixed bayonets, or by midshipmen with loaded pistols.

The magazines were situated in the fore and after parts of the ship's hold. They were far below water, and situated in midships, so that no shot could penetrate to them. They were lit by ingenious contrivances called light-rooms, small chambers built just forward of them, and separated from them by double windows of glass. Lanterns were lit in these light-rooms and placed behind the windows, so that their light should illuminate the magazines. The floors or decks of the magazines were covered with felt, or with a rough kind of frieze known as fearnought. The walls or sides were similarly covered. No man was allowed to enter them until he had covered his shoes with thick felt slippers, and emptied his pockets of any steel or other metal, the striking of which might make a spark. The after-magazine was the smaller of the two. It contained no powder casks, but only a store of filled cartridges for the supply of the upper-deck 18- and 24-pounders, and the forecastle and quarter-deck carronades. In the fore-magazine were the tiers of powder casks, one above the other, the lowest tier having copper hoops about them. This place was protected even more carefully than the after-magazine, for here the loose powder was handled and placed in cartridge; and here the hand grenades and musket cartridges were stored. Here, too, were the cartridges ready filled for the batteries of 32-pounders on the lower or first gun-deck. This magazine was not reached by direct descent from a ladder. To reach it one had to pass along a little passage protected by a copper door and guarded by a marine. The cartridges for the cannon were stored in cylindrical wooden tubs or boxes, arranged in racks and covered with movable wooden lids. Forward of the fore-magazine was a lift or hoist, by which the cartridges could be passed from the magazine to the orlop, so that the boys employed in passing powder should not have to descend into the magazine. In some ships there was no such hoist, but a thick, wet, woollen screen with a hole in it, through which the cartridges were handed. The boys employed in carrying powder had to cover the cartridges with their jackets as they ran from the magazine to the gun they supplied. All magazines were fitted with a water tank and pipes, by which the chamber could be swamped in the event of fire.

Between the magazines was the vast round belly of the ship, known as the hold. Here the ballast, provision casks, and water casks were stowed. In the space forward of the after-magazine was a chamber known as the fish-room, for the storage of the ship's salt fish. Beside it was the spirit-room, full of wine, brandy, and rum casks. Farther forward was the bread-room, a large apartment lined with tin, and artificially dried by hanging stoves. It contained an incredible quantity of ship's biscuit, of which a pound a day was allowed to each man on board. The water and beer casks, and the casks containing peas, oatmeal, and salt flesh were stowed forward of the bread-room, according to the rules of the service.

13

Chapter II

The guns in use in our Navy / Their nature
How loaded and fired / varieties / Carronades / Shot
Small arms / Gun ports

The cannon with which Nelson's ships were armed were made of brass or iron. The iron guns were cast in a mould, and then bored, or tubed by the insertion of a powerful cylindrical gouge. They do not appear to have been cast round a core. The brass guns were made of a proportion of "metal fit for casting" (generally about five-sevenths of the whole), to which was added a seventh part of copper, a rather similar quantity of brass, and a few pounds of tin. The exact proportions were kept secret by the founders. German founders used more tin than brass, while the French used two formulae, in both of which more tin than brass was employed.

The guns in use in our service were distinguished and named by the weight of the balls they threw. The old names of demi-cannon, saker, curtal, cannon-perier, etc., had fallen out of use. The guns were spoken of as 6-, 12-, 18-, 24-, or 32-pounders. The 32-pounder was the largest gun in use. Until 1790 a ponderous gun, throwing a 42-pound shot, had been mounted on ships of the line, but the gun was too unwieldy, and the shock of the discharge was too great to allow of its continued use. There were, however, 42-, and even 68-pounder carronade or 'smasher' guns. These were mounted on improved carriages, the invention of Admiral Bertie. The principal parts of a 32-pounder gun were the breech, which ended in a rounded iron ball called the pomelion, or cascabel; the trunnions or extended arms, which supported the cannon (in almost perfect balance) in its carriage; and the bore or calibre, the "concave cylinder" down which the charge was rammed. The trunnions were placed, not in the centre of the piece but rather towards the breech, as the metal at the breech was thicker and heavier than at the mouth, to withstand the shock of explosion, and to prevent the gun from "starting up behind" when fired. The bore was, of course, of the same size throughout. "Taper-bored" guns had fallen out of favour. All guns in use were mounted on strong wooden trucks or carriages. The carriages were composed of two "cheeks" or side pieces, held together by thick wooden cross pieces and iron axle-trees. The wheels on which the carriages rested were circular discs of strong wood, held to the axle by iron linch-pins. The trunnions of the guns rested on the top of the two cheeks, directly above the front wheels. They were placed in hollows cut to receive them, over which hinged iron clamps or cap-squares passed, to keep them from jolting out at the shock of the discharge.

When placed on a carriage, and resting on its trunnions, the gun inclined to sag down towards its breech. It was kept from falling out of the horizontal position by a wedge of wood, called a coin (or quoin) which rested on the bed of the carriage. The withdrawal of the wedge caused the gun to elevate its muzzle. By means of graduated scales, cut upon the coins and upon the base-rings of the guns, the gunners could elevate or depress their piece with considerable accuracy, by the insertion and withdrawal of the supporting wedges.

At sea, where the ship was in continual motion, either rolling or pitching, the guns had to be secured with great care by means of tackles and breechings. These ropes enabled the gun's crews to work their guns in action. A breeching was made of stout hemp rope of the finest quality. It passed through a ring or "thimble," which was strapped to the round iron ball or pomelion of the gun.[1] The ends of it were secured or "clinched" to strong iron ring-bolts in the ship's side, one at each side of the gun port. This breeching secured the gun from rolling backwards towards the inner part of the deck, while it checked the recoil of the piece when fired. A breeching was of such a length that, when the piece was fired, it checked the recoil directly the gun muzzle was immediately within the gun port. In this position the piece could be reloaded without difficulty. The gun or side-tackles were pulleys hooked to the sides of the carriages, and to ring-bolts in the ship's side, to enable the gun's crews to run the piece out when they had loaded it. The gun was kept from running out of itself with the roll of the ship by a tackle, called a train or preventer tackle, which was hooked to an iron ring-bolt in midships, and to a hook directly below the breech of the gun.[2] When not in action the guns were hauled close up to the ship's side by means of the side-tackles. The two parts of the breeching were then lashed together, to allow no possible play to the piece. The coins were taken out, so that the muzzle of the gun just touched the upper part of the gun port, to which it was lashed with a length of cord. In very bad weather, when the ship's rolling caused the guns to strain their fastenings, the tackles and breechings were doubled, and small wooden wedges were screwed under their wheels. A gun broken loose was a very terrible engine of destruction, for the two tons of iron, flying across the deck with the roll of the ship, would strike with fearful force against the opposite side. Such a force was more than likely to tear through the timbers, carrying with it any other gun it happened to strike. If a gun broke loose it was "tripped" or upset by hammocks or spare sails flung in its path. but the task of tripping a loose gun on a deck awash with the sea, and foul with all manner of floating gear, such as rammers and buckets, was by no means an easy one. It was like playing leap-frog on a see-saw under a shower bath, with the certainty of a horrible death if you missed your leap.

When secured to the ship's side, and at all times when not in action, the muzzle of a gun was stopped with a circular plug of wood or cork, known as a tompion.[3]

1   *This ring or thimble was sometimes cast on the piece above the pomelion*

2   *As the natural roll of the ship was more marked on the lee side, the lee guns were always fitted with strong train tackles, which were strained taut by one of the crew of each gun*

3   *The tompion was secured to the gun muzzle by a lanyard. It was generally painted red, with a gilt cross.*

15

This plug was carefully tallowed round its outer rim so that no water should pass by it into the bore of the piece. Over the touch-hole of the gun, when not in action, a thin sheet of lead was fixed. This sheet was about a foot square, and was known as the "apron" because it was tied to its place by two white cords. It kept the vent or touch-hole dry, and defended the priming from chance ignition.[1]

Above the guns, hooked to the beams, so as to be out of the way when not in use, were the implements for loading and cleaning. A gun was loaded in the following manner: The powder was inserted by means of a ladle — a sort of copper shovel — with a long wooden handle. The head of this shovel resembled a "cylindrical spoon." Into its cavity the cartridge fitted, so that the loader had but to thrust the ladle down and turn it over to deposit the cartridge in its place at the extremity of the bore. A wad of rope yarn was then driven home upon the charge by an implement known as the rammer. The shot was then rammed home, with a wad on top of it.[2] The tightness or looseness of this, the containing wad, did not affect the velocity of the cannon ball. As a rule, therefore, the upper wad was driven in with force just sufficient to keep the shot in the gun while aim was taken. Tight wads were seldom used, as they took too long to drive down the muzzle.

When the piece was loaded the captain of the gun took out his priming-iron, an implement like a knitting-needle, with a few spirals (as in a corkscrew) at the end. This he thrust down the touch-hole into the cartridge, so that the iron not only cleared the vent, but also cut through the cartridge. He then opened his priming-box and took out a priming-tube, which was either of tin or of quill, and, in either case, of less than one-fifth of an inch in diameter. This he placed in the touch-hole, so that the sharp end of it entered into the cartridge. Priming-tubes were filled with the very best mealed powder, "mixed up stiff with spirits of wine." Their upper ends were frayed, so that the fire might reach them the more readily. If there were no priming-tubes the captain of the gun primed his piece from a powder-horn, by merely pouring good mealed powder down the touch-hole, and then laying a little train of the same along a channel cut in the gun for the purpose. This little groove led from the vent towards the breech of the piece. The powder placed in this groove was always slightly bruised with the end of the powder-horn. When the gun was primed and aimed, the captain of the piece watched his opportunity to fire, taking care to fire as his side of the ship rose slowly[3] from a roll, so that his shot, if it missed the ship he aimed at, might yet cut her rigging. The piece was fired, as a rule, by means of a match, or length, of twisted cotton wicks soaked in lye, which burned very slowly, and remained

---

1   *In 1812 one of the main-deck guns of H.M.S. Bacchante discharged itself suddenly, without apparent cause. The leaden apron was in its place, no fire had been near the gun, and no violent concussion had shaken the ship. The ball killed a midshipman, and narrowly missed the captain of a flagship. The cause of the explosion was never discovered. See 'Donat O'Brien's Adventures,' p. 321. Ed. 1902*

2   *When the gun fired red-hot shot, as in many general actions, the wad driven down upon the powder was a disc of green wood, wrapped about with yarns.*

3   *The French invariably fired as the ship rose from a roll. Some English Admirals preferred to fire as the ship began to roll so that the shot might strike the hull of the enemy either above or below the water line.*

alight when once lit for several hours. Matches in actual use were twisted about a forked staff some three feet long, which was known as the linstock.[1] Immediately before a battle matches ready for use were placed between the guns in tubs, known as match tubs, which were half filled with sand or water. The matches were fixed in notches in the rim of each tub, so that their burning ends overhung the water or sand. Their loose ends lay upon the deck. When a man gave fire to a piece he held the burning match below the level of the vent, and blew on the lighted end to make it burn clearly. At the favourable instant he applied the red end to the train of powder leading to the touch-hole, and then smartly drew back the linstock to avoid the "huff" or spit of fire from the vent at the moment of explosion. The spirt of flame was sufficiently violent to blow the linstock out of a man's hand if he applied it carelessly. It also burnt pockmarks on the beams directly above the gun, so that in many old wooden men-of-war the beams were deeply pitted all along the deck. After 1780 the guns of some ships were fitted with flint-locks, by means of which a spark struck from a flint was thrown on to the pan or tube containing the priming powder. The triggers of these locks were released by a smart pull upon a lanyard. These flint-locks were safer than the old arrangement of match and powder train. They were also more certain and more easily managed. Their use enabled the gunners to fire more rapidly, but the sailors disliked them, and the captains looked upon them as dangerous innovations, opposed to the old traditions of the service. They were not generally adopted until after the battle of the Nile. A ship employing them in that engagement made such excellent and such rapid practice that the seamen were convinced of their merit. A flint-lock was, however, always liable to lose its flint, either by fracture or by being stricken from its place. Many guns were fitted with double or even treble flints so that the breaking or slipping of a single stone should not stop the fire. Until long after Nelson's death it was the rule for ships going into action to carry lighted matches in match tubs between the guns, for use if the flint-locks missed fire.

The gun when fired recoiled with great violence to the limit of the breeching. When a gun had become hot from continuous firing the violence of its recoil became so great that the carriage would be lifted from the deck, and the whole contrivance would leap to the beams above at each shot. The breechings used to snap like twine under the tremendous strain of such recoils, particularly on the lower-deck, where the ropes were frequently wetted and subject to rot. In general actions the guns were fitted with double-breechings to prevent such ruptures.

The recoil of the gun was very dangerous to the gun's crews, for no man, however experienced, could predict, from the direction in which the gun pointed and the motion of the ship, in what way the gun would run back. Numbers of men were killed or wounded by the recoil of guns, and no device checked the evil altogether, though several inventions modified it. The breeching always kept it within certain bounds, while it was checked naturally by the slope of the deck, from in midships, towards the ship's sides.

1 *More frequently they were held in the hand.*

When a gun had been fired successfully[1] it recoiled into the position for reloading. Before a fresh cartridge was thrust down the muzzle, an instrument called a worm, a sort of large edged corkscrew, was sometimes inserted to scrape out any burning scraps which might remain in the gun. With some kinds of cartridges this was necessary after each discharge. When the worm had been passed, a sponge was thrust down, and twisted round once or twice as soon as its head had reached the end of the bore. By the time the gun had been sponged, and the sponge tapped out, a fresh cartridge was ready for insertion. The head of a sponge was usually of rough sheepskin wool affixed to a stout piece of rope, stiffened with spun yarn, at the other end of which was a wooden butt, studded with copper, for use as a rammer. A rope handle was found far safer than one of wood, for it allowed the sailor to bend it, so that he could pass it down the gun without leaning out of the port, as a mark for the enemy's sharp-shooters. In sponging and ramming the sailor showed himself as little as possible. If he had to expose himself at the port as he sponged, he always held the sponge away from the ship's side, with his body between it and the timbers, so that if a shot struck the handle it might not force the implement through his body.

The guns were trained aft and forward by means of handspikes or wooden levers, which were sometimes fitted with iron claws. With these the carriage of a gun could be shifted, little by little, in the required direction. The handspikes were also used to raise the breech of the gun, when the gun captain adjusted the piece to the required height by means of the coins. In raising the breech, the sailor used as his fulcrum one of the steps cut in the cheek or side of the gun-carriage. The work of shifting one of these heavy guns by such a clumsy contrivance was very hard. In action the men stripped to their waists, yet a very few minutes of the work sufficed to make them hot. The exercise was so violent that in hot engagements the men sometimes fell exhausted beside their guns and slept there in all the uproar of the fight.

The guns generally in use were cast in two lengths, "long" and "short," both varieties having about the same range, but with this difference. The long gun was more accurate, and could be laid point blank — that is, level or horizontal — to fire at an object at a distance, say, of 300 yards. To hit the same object at that distance a short gun had to be slightly elevated, and the more the gun was elevated the less accurate it became. The short gun was the more popular in the years of which we write, for it was more destructive at close quarters, and commanders preferred to come to close quarters before engaging. In the American War of 1812 this preference for the short gun lost us several frigates. The American frigates which captured them were armed with long guns. With these they were able to remain aloof, plying our ships with shot at long range; while the short guns aboard our ships replied inaccurately, their shot falling short or missing, owing to the great elevation necessary to make them carry the distance.

1 *Misfires were not infrequent. The priming powder sometimes fizzled and smoked, without setting fire to the charge. On these occasions the gun's crew stood aloof till all appearance of smoke had faded from the touch-hole, when the captain crept up cautiously, cleaned out the vent, and reprimed the gun.*

18

The following table may help the reader to understand the sizes and qualifications of the guns in use:—

Calibre	Length of Piece	Length of Bore	Weight of Gun	Charge of Powder	Point-Blank Range	Extreme Range at 10° Elevation
32-pr. long	9ft. 6 ins.	8 ft. 11 ins	55 cwt. 2 qrs.	11-10 lbs.	350 yards	2900 yards
32-pr. short	8 ft	7 ft. 6 ins	49 " 3 "	"	"	"
24-pr. long	9 ft. 6 ins.	8 ft. 11 ins	50 "	8-4 lbs.	297-265 yards	2870-2513 yards
"	9 ft.	8 ft. 5½ ins.	47 " 2 "	"	"	"
"	8 ft.	7 ft. 5½ ins.	43 " 2 "	"	"	"
24-pr. short	7 ft. 6 ins.	6 ft. 11 ins.	40 "	6-4 lbs.	288-221 yards.	2668-2562 yards
"	6 ft 6 ins.	6 ft. 11 ins	33 "	"	"	"
"	6 ft.	5 ft. 11 ins	31 "	"	"	"
"	9 ft.	8 ft. 6 ins.	42 """	8-4 lbs.	297-265 yards	2870-2513 yards
"	8 ft.	7 ft. 6 ins.	37 "	"	"	"
18-pr. short	6 ft.	5 ft. 6 ins.	27 "	6-4 lbs.	288-221 yards	2668-2562 yards
12-pr. long	9 ft.	8 ft. 6¼ ins.	34 "	3½ lbs.	300 yards	1800 yards at most at 6° elevation
"	8 ft. 6 ins.	8 ft.	33 "	"	"	"
12-pr. short	7 ft. 6 ins.	7 ft.	29 "	"	"	"
9-pr. long	9 ft.	8 ft. 6 ins.	31 "	"	"	"
"	8 ft. 6 ins.	8 ft. 6 ins.	28 "	3 lbs.	"	"
9-pr. short	7 ft. 6 ins.	7 ft.	26 "	"	"	"
"	7 ft.	6 ft. 6 ins.	25 "	"	"	"

19

The guns at sea were invariably kept loaded, but the charges were frequently drawn, as the powder deteriorated if left too long in the gun. In action, when not in use, the crows, handspikes, rammers, etc., were laid on the deck near the ship's side. After an engagement the sponges and rammers were hooked to the ship's beams, above the gun. In action, the priming-horn was hung to the beams between shots. After action it was returned to the gunner and stored away in one of the magazines. Each gun was fought by a gun's crew of from eight to four men according to the size of the piece.

The guns were generally painted a sort of grey-blue steel colour, with a scarlet band round the muzzle.[1] Some captains merely blackened their guns. Others blackened them, and kept the brass sights and steel cap-squares polished. These were, however, in the minority until 1811. One or two captains painted their guns a pure white. After 1811 the custom of "spit and polish" began, to the great misery of the sailors. Until that time the bright work of the guns was generally painted over.

The carronade guns, which were mounted on all ships in addition to their regulation iron ordnance, were the invention of a Mr Gascoine. They were named after the town in Scotland where they were first cast. They first came into use in 1779. They were short, squat guns, ranging from about five to two feet in length, and flinging balls of from 6 to 12 lbs. in weight. They were lighter than the ordinary guns, and were therefore useful for the quarter-deck, and spar-deck batteries. They were easily managed, and a crew of four men could work the heaviest of them. They were mounted on sliding wooden carriages traversing on a wheel, while the gun was so fixed upon the carriage that it would slide in or out as desired. They were not elevated by handspikes, like the iron main-batteries, for a screw which passed through the iron pomelion gave them their elevation or depression. The coins could be used to give extraordinary depression if such were needed.

Being very short, the point-blank range of a carronade was small, varying from 450 to 230 yards, according to the size of the gun. At an elevation of 4°, at which a 32-pounder gun would carry nearly a mile, the 32-pounder carronade carried less than 1000 yards. But at close quarters the carronade was a much more terrible weapon than any gun mounted on the lower-deck. At a short distance it made such fearful havoc of a ship's side that it was called the "smasher" or "devil-gun." It had several very serious defects. It was so short a piece that, when run out, it barely cleared the sill of its port. To fire it in that position endangered the rigging and ship's side, though no case has been reported of a ship having been set on fire by the discharge of a carronade. Another serious defect was the violence of the recoil, which sometimes split the carriage and dismounted the gun. Admiral Bertie's invention modified this evil, but never overcame it. Carronades were loaded and fired in precisely the same way as iron guns of the lower batteries.

The shot fired by guns and carronades was usually spherical or "round-shot," made of cast iron. Leaden round-shot was sometimes used, apparently with great effect, but the cost was too great to admit of its general use. A store of round-shot, scraped

1 *Guns were often painted red to match the carriages and ship's sides.*

1 *Guns were often painted red to match the carriages and ship's sides.*

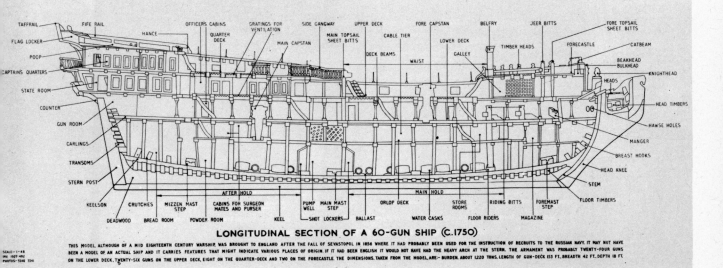

TAFFRAIL · FIFE RAIL · HANCE · OFFICERS CABINS · QUARTER DECK · GRATINGS FOR VENTILATION · SIDE GANGWAY · UPPER DECK · FORE CAPSTAN · BELFRY · JEER BITTS · FORE TOPSAIL SHEET BITTS

FLAG LOCKER · MAIN CAPSTAN · MAIN TOPSAIL SHEET BITTS · CABLE TIER · LOWER DECK · TIMBER HEADS · FORECASTLE · CATBEAM

POOP · DECK BEAMS · WAIST · GALLEY · BEAKHEAD BULKHEAD

CAPTAINS QUARTERS · HEADS · KNIGHTHEAD

STATE ROOM · HEAD TIMBERS

COUNTER · HAWSE HOLES

GUN ROOM · MANGER

CARLINGS · BREAST HOOKS

TRANSOMS · HEAD KNEE

STERN POST · STEM

AFTER HOLD · MAIN HOLD · FLOOR TIMBERS

KEELSON · CRUTCHES · MIZZEN MAST STEP · CABINS FOR SURGEON MATES AND PURSER · PUMP WELL · MAIN MAST STEP · ORLOP DECK · STORE ROOMS · RIDING BITTS · FOREMAST STEP

DEADWOOD · BREAD ROOM · POWDER ROOM · KEEL · SHOT LOCKERS · BALLAST · WATER CASKS · FLOOR RIDERS · MAGAZINE

LONGITUDINAL SECTION OF A 60-GUN SHIP (C.1750)

SCALE:- 1"·48
INV. 1927·492
PHOTOS:- 3340 3341

THIS MODEL, ALTHOUGH OF A MID EIGHTEENTH CENTURY WARSHIP, WAS BROUGHT TO ENGLAND AFTER THE FALL OF SEVASTOPOL IN 1856 WHERE IT HAD PROBABLY BEEN USED FOR THE INSTRUCTION OF RECRUITS TO THE RUSSIAN NAVY. IT MAY NOT HAVE
BEEN A MODEL OF AN ACTUAL SHIP AND IT CARRIES FEATURES THAT MIGHT INDICATE VARIOUS PLACES OF ORIGIN. IF IT HAD BEEN ENGLISH IT WOULD NOT HAVE HAD THE HEAVY ARCH AT THE STERN. THE ARMAMENT WAS PROBABLY TWENTY-FOUR GUNS
ON THE LOWER DECK, TWENTY-SIX GUNS ON THE UPPER DECK, EIGHT ON THE QUARTER-DECK AND TWO ON THE FORECASTLE. THE DIMENSIONS, TAKEN FROM THE MODEL, ARE:- BURDEN ABOUT 1220 TONS, LENGTH OF GUN-DECK 153 FT., BREADTH 42 FT., DEPTH 18 FT.

Plate 1. *Contemporary model of a 60 gun ship built about 1750. Such a ship required about 2000 oak trees in its construction. The Victory was completed about 15 years later.*

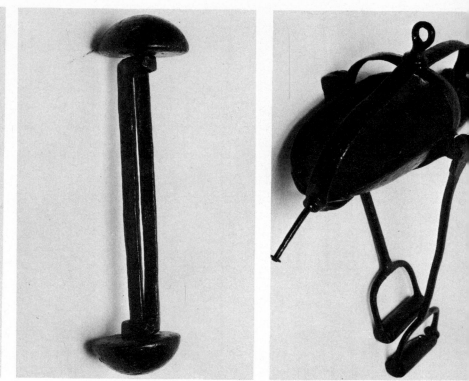

GRAPE SHOT

This particular type consisted of
three tiers of cast iron balls, seperated
by parallel iron discs and connected by
a central pin. The whole was enclosed
in a canvas bag, bound tightly round
with rope

Plate 2(a) *Bar shot of the small dumb-bell type.*
(b) Elongating shot. On emerging from the muzzle this type of shot almost doub-led its effective length.
(c) Shot carrier. In attempting to set the enemy ship on fire, round shot were brought to white heat in furnaces.
(d) Grape shot. Shot of this type consisted of 3 tiers of iron balls, separated by parallel iron discs and connected by a central pin. The whole was enclosed in a canvas bag, bound tightly round with rope.
(e) Chain shot – used for destroying the enemy's rigging.

very clean, was always carried in the shot racks on the gun-decks. These shot were kept free from rust by paint or grease. Shot were sometimes so thickly coated with rust, when brought from the hold, that they would not enter the muzzles of the guns for which they were cast. The officers generally endeavoured to keep fifteen or twenty rounds of shot scraped clean in order to avoid the use of rusty balls until the brunt of the fight was over. In close action another kind of shot was used as a scourer or murderer. This was grape shot, "a combination of balls," weighing each 2 lbs., which were packed up in cylindrical canvas bags, of the size of the cannon ball generally used for the gun. A bag of 16 iron balls was used for a 32-pounder, of 12 for a 24-pounder, and of 9 for an 18-pounder. The bags were strongly corded into their cylindrical shape. These 2-lb. iron balls could cut through chain, so that a discharge of them often helped to bring down an enemy's mast, by cutting the stays and standing rigging. In hot actions, when the ships lay "yard-arm to yard-arm," close alongside each other, every second gun was loaded with bags of grape-shot, because "in any close action they are capable of committing infinite ravages against both men and material." To clear an enemy's decks at close range, a kind of shot called case or canister was sometimes used. This was made of leaden musket and pistol bullets, or of shot of half-a-pound weight, packed up tightly in tin cylinders. At very close range this sort of shot committed most ghastly massacre, but it could not be used at a distance of more than 200 yards, as the shot scattered over a wide area, and so lost its effect. Chain shot, or two balls linked together by an iron chain, was used to bring down masts and spars. Bar shot, or two half-round shot joined by a bar was sometimes used, particularly by the French. Bar shot were often frapped about with combustibles, which ignited when the gun was fired, and so set fire to the sails or hull of the opposing ship. Langrel, or langridge, was a collection of old iron, nuts, bolts, bars, and scraps of chain, tied by rope yarns into "a sort of a cylinder," and so fired at masts and rigging. Dismantling shot or shot made of half-a-dozen iron bars, "each about two feet long, fastened by ring-heads to a strong ring," was most efficacious in tearing off sails, and bringing down masts and spars. In close action, and when the guns grew hot, the charges of powder were always reduced by at least a third. When the ships lay close together, the charges were made very small, because shot which barely penetrated a ship's timber occasioned "the greatest shake," and tore off "the greatest number of, and largest, splinters." As splinters were nearly always more terrible (and more feared) than shot, the gunners did their best to produce them. In some ships the opening broadsides were fired with light charges in order that the bullets might shatter the enemy's timber and send the splinters flying.

The small-arms in general use in the Navy were the musket, the musketoon, the pistol, the cutlass, the boarding-pike, the axe or tomahawk, the bayonet, the sailor's knife, and the midshipman's dirk. The musket was the weapon of the marines. It was a flint-lock, muzzle-loading, smooth-bore, firing a ball of from 1 to 2 ounces, with a charge of 4½ drachms of powder. It could be fired with comparative certainty at any object within 100 yards. Its extreme range may have been a quarter of a mile. It

21

sometimes killed at 200 yards. Its barrel was ¾ of an inch in diameter. Its length, from muzzle to pan, was 3 feet 6 inches. The musketeer carried his cartridges in a box. In loading he had to bite off the bullet from the top of the cartridge, so as to expose the powder. He then sprinkled a little of the powder into the pan of the gun, snapped the pan to, dropped the cartridge down the muzzle, rammed it home, with the bullet on top, and then took aim and fired. The sailors were drilled in the use of the musket whenever the opportunity offered.

The musketoon was a short heavy musket with a big bore. It threw a ball weighing from 5 to 7½ ounces. It was only used at close quarters. Some musketoons had bell mouths, like blunderbusses. They kicked very dangerously, but were most effective in repelling boarders.

There were various kinds of pistols in use, some of them of more than one barrel. The boarders, or men told off from each gun to board an enemy's ship, if occasion served, were always supplied with at least two pistols for use at close-quarters. They were loaded with cartridges, which had to be bitten like the cartridges of the muskets. A boarder, in the rush and hurry of the hand-to-hand fighting, had never time to reload after he had emptied his pistol barrels. He flung the weapons away immediately he had burned his cartridges, and laid about him with his cutlass, boarding-axe, or boarding-pike. As a last resource he had always his sailor's knife. The cutlass was a curved heavy cutting sword, about 3 feet long, with a black japanned hilt and basket-guard. The axe was a small heavy axe, with a short steel head and a projecting spike. It was used less as a weapon than as a tool for cutting the lanyards of stays and shrouds, the running rigging, etc. etc. The boarding-pike or half-pike was a spike of steel fixed on a staff of ash. It was a very useful tool for the driving back of boarders. Rows of them, diversified with tomahawks, were sometimes placed along the poop and forecastle, with the hafts scraped clean, and the steels blackened. The other small-arms, such as pistols and cutlasses, were stored in arm-chests in different parts of the ship, and in stands about the masts below decks. Sergeants of marines still carried halberds or whole pikes, about 8 feet long, with heads which combined the spear and axe, "so that they serve equally to cut down or push withal." With these instruments the sergeants aligned their files at muster or inspection. As supplementary weapons some ships carried small swivel guns in the tops aloft, to scour the upper-decks and tops of the enemy at close range. A gun of this kind threw a shot of half - a - pound weight. It mounted on an iron crotch, and had a long handle in place of a cascabel, by which it could be turned and pointed.

Before closing this description of the naval armaments in use we must give some short account of the gun ports. A gun port was a square opening in the ship's side, fitted with a heavy, hinged wooden lid opening outward. When closed, this lid was hooked to an iron bar to keep it from swinging outward as the ship rolled. To open a port one had to haul upon a rope, called a port-tackle, which led from the inside of the ship through a round hole above the port, and thence down to a ring on the outside of the lid. When the ports were open to admit the air the guns were sometimes fitted with "half-ports" or wooden screens, through which their muzzles pointed but which kept out most of the spray which dashed against the sides. The hinges of the port-lids were protected from wet by little semicircular slips of wood arched just above them. These slips were known as port-riggles. The carpenters were expected to attend to the opening and lowering of the ports, so that the lids, when opened, might all make the same angle from the ship's side.

In some ships the centres of the port-lids were fitted with thick glass bull's-eyes, which admitted light when the ports were battened in.

Chapter III

The quarter-deck officers / The Captain /
The lieutenants / The master, second master, and
master's mates / The midshipmen / The midshipman's berth

The captain[1] of a man-of-war, on receiving his appointment to a ship, at once repaired on board her, wherever she then lay, first obtaining from the master-attendant of the dockyard a new narrow pendant, a swallow-tailed piece of red-and-white bunting to hoist at her masthead. Having repaired on board, and hoisted his pendant, the captain read his commission, or "read himself in," before the caretakers and old seamen aboard the ship. He then set about fitting her for the sea (if she were a new ship) with all possible dispatch; and an Admiralty Order forbade his sleeping ashore, without express permission from his superiors, until his ship was paid off. He had to examine all guns, gun-carriages, muskets, cutlasses, and small-arms when they were hoisted on board, and to reject any faulty weapon. He had to keep inventories of all stores sent aboard, and counterparts of the inventories of his warrant officers—such as those of the boatswain and gunner. He kept an account of the ship's provisions, showing the daily expenditure of junk and spirits. He had "to use his best endeavours to get the ship manned," by the dispersal of alluring placards all over the town near which he lay, promising "quick promotion, heaps of prize-money, free rations," etc. etc. to all who would enter. He was also expected to open a rendezvous at a sailor's tavern, where the master-at-arms and coxswain could blarney sailors into joining. Sometimes he was able to offer a bounty or money-reward to every seaman who entered. If neither sugary announcements nor the offer of a piece of gold could lure men to the living death of a gun-deck he had to have recourse to the press. He would send his boats ashore after dark, in command of lieutenants or master's mates, to search the dockside brothels and sailors' taverns. Any sailors or seafaring folk discovered in these haunts were dragged from the arms of their trulls and taken aboard. Often the press-gangs had to fight to bring off their men, for the women and bullies sometimes rallied to the rescue. Many a bold lieutenant had his cheeks scratched or his hair pulled out, and many a bold tarrybreeks got his head broken in these encounters. The gangs never took firearms on these excursions, but contented

1 *It is hardly necessary to say that a captain was junior to a commodore, or senior captain, and to an admiral or flag officer. The admiral commanded squadrons of ships; the commodore, detachments from those squadrons. The present work is of too narrow a scope to allow of any consideration of their respective duties. We must confine ourselves to an account of the usual officers aboard a ship of war. Those curious to learn about commodore and admiral will find plenty of information in Burney's "Falconer," and the various Naval Histories.*

24

themselves with stretchers and cudgels (such as wooden belaying pins). They generally carried cutlasses, but "more for their majesty to astonish the enemy," than for actual use.

Press-gangs made great havoc among watermen and dockside labourers. They were expected primarily to capture sailors and seafaring people, but "a man-of-war, like a gallows, refused nothing," and any landsmen served their turn. They were, at least, "mortal men," and did as well as any others to stop a bullet or to feed powder. Marryat mentions a ship which was manned by the men of nineteen nations, professing among them, some fifty-seven different trades. Tailors, little tradesmen, street loafers, all were fair game. They were taken to the boats and sent aboard, and cracked across the heads with a cudgel if they protested. When once on board they were shoved down below-decks, under a marine sentry who had orders to shoot them if they attempted to escape. When convenient the captain examined these wretches, as to their fitness for the sea-service. He had them examined by the surgeon, to make sure that they were not infested nor infected. Any man who appeared to be too sickly for the work was discharged. A dirty man was cleaned, and his clothes fumigated. Apprentices who could produce their indentures, or merchant-sailors who could claim exemption, were dismissed. All the others were carefully retained. Many pressed men made the best of a very hard bargain by offering to ship within a fortnight of their impressment. Those who acted thus were allowed the King's bounty, and won for themselves (to some extent) the good opinion of the officers.

This way of impressing folk was but one of the ways by which a captain could get his fleet manned. Men condemned at the sessions were sometimes offered the hard alternative of the gallows or service afloat. Often they chose the greater of the two evils. Absconding debtors, and those pursued by the redbreasts, or Bow Street Runners, were frequently eager to ship to avoid capture. A number of men shipped because they had had their heads turned by sea-songs or similar cant, describing the beauty of life afloat, etc. Large numbers were sent from London by the Lord Mayor. These were generally young bloods or bucks, who had been found drunk in the streets or bawdy houses, and feared to see their names in the police-magistrates' lists, and police-court reports. They were known as "my Lord Mayor's men," and very bad bargains they generally were. It was reckoned that one-third of each ship's company was composed of landsmen, and that one-eighth of the entire number of men serving in His Majesty's ships were foreigners.

Having got a crew together by these gentle means, the captain had to see to it that each man's name was entered in the ship's books, particularly the muster book, in which a sort of prison record was kept to enable the officers to identify deserters. The colours of a man's hair and eyes were noted. His chest measurement was taken. His tattoo marks were described. If the man deserted, these particulars were sent to the Admiralty, with an account of the escape. The muster books were kept with great care, and submitted every month or two months to the Admiralty. They contained among other matter the records of any deductions to be made from the pay of the members of the crew.

25

At sea the captain was responsible for the ship, and for all on board her. He had to see that the lieutenant made out his quarter bills allotting the hands to their stations. He kept the keys of the magazines, and saw to it that sentries guarded those places, to prevent the entry of unauthorised persons. He had to be vigilant to prevent all possibility of fire, by forbidding candles in the cable tiers or at the breaking out of spirits from the spirit-room. He was to order all lights out at 8 p.m. each night. He was to forbid smoking "in any other place than the galley." He was to see the men exercised at the great guns, and with their small-arms. He had to see that the colours were "not kept abroad in windy weather." He had to keep a journal in duplicate, for the benefit of the Admiralty; and at the end of a cruise he had to send an account "of the qualities of his ship" to the commissioners. He had charge of the sea-stores known as slops, such as bedding and clothing, which he sold to those of the crew who needed them. He had to keep his ship clean, dry, and well ventilated, by having the decks swept and scrubbed, the ports opened, the wells and bilges pumped, and windsails (or ventilators) fitted to expel the foul air from the hold. He was to punish transgressors, discourage vice and immorality, defend his country's honour, keep secret the private signals, and "burn, sink, and destroy" as much of the enemy as he could. These are but a few of the forty-eight duties required of him.

The captain's share of prize-money was "three-eighth parts" of the value of the prize. His pay varied from about 6s. to 25s. a day, in accordance with the importance of his command. The captain of a 74 received 13s. 6d. a day. Until 1794, he was allowed to have four servants for every 100 men aboard his ship, a regulation which afforded him an opportunity to provide for his friends and poor relations. A captain in the old time frequently put to sea with a little band of parasites about him. They stuck to him as jackals stick to the provident lion, following him from ship to ship, living on his bounty, and thriving on his recommendations. When one reads of a distinguished naval officer having been "a captain's servant," it does not mean that he blacked the captain's boots, mixed his grog, and emptied his slops, but that he entered the service under a captain's protection. Nelson was a "captain's servant" to Captain Maurice Suckling on the guard ship at Chatham, but he was very far from being Captain Suckling's flunkey. The system was bad, and much abused, but it lingered until 1794, when it was abolished, and a money compensation paid to the captains. It had been attended with a curious privilege. A captain removing from one ship to another was allowed to carry with him not only his servants, but his boat's crew, his coxswain, some of his warrant officers, his clerk and purser, and a number of able seamen. From a first-rate ship he could take, in all, 80 men; from a second-rate, 65; from a third-rate, 50; from a fourth-rate, 40; from a fifth-rate, 20; and from a sixth-rate, 10.

Those who have trembled under the command of a sea captain will not need to be told of his powers and dignities. A captain of a ship at sea is not only a commander, but a judge of the supreme court, and a kind of human parallel to Deity. "He is a Leviathan," says the scurrilous Ward, "or rather a kind of Sea-God, whom the poor tars worship as the Indians do the Devil." There was no appeal from a sentence pronounced by such a one. His word was absolute. He had power over his subjects almost to the life. That he could not touch, without the consent of his equals, but he had the power to flog a man senseless, and authority to break some of his officers and send them forward. He had power to loose and to bind, and perhaps no single man has ever held such authority over the fortunes of his subordinates as that held by a sea captain over his company at sea during the Napoleonic wars. He lived alone, like a little god in a heaven, shrouded from view by the cabin bulkheads, and guarded always by a red-coated sentry, armed with a drawn sword. If he came on deck the lieutenants at once shifted over to the lee side, out of respect to the great man. No man on board dared to address him, save on some question relating to the duty of the day. No sailor could speak to him with his hat upon his head. One uncovered to one's captain as to one's God. When he came aboard, after a visit to the shore, he was received with honour. The "side-boys," dressed in white, rigged the green or red side-ropes to the gangway, and stood there, at attention, to await his arrival. The boatswain, in his uniform, went to the gangway to "pipe the side"—that is, to blow a solemn salute upon his whistle—as the august foot came on to the deck. The marine sentry stood to attention, A number of midshipmen and other officers and men fell in upon the quarter-deck. The ship became as silent as the tomb, save for the slow solemn piping of the boatswain. The captain stepped on board, saluted the quarter-deck, and passed aft to his cabin, generally paying not the very least attention to the assembled worshippers. The same ceremony was performed when the captain left the ship.

The captain stood no watch, and did not interfere with the ordinary working of the ship until something went wrong. He lived alone in his cabin, eating in solitude, save when he desired his lieutenants and midshipmen to dine with him. On these occasions he graciously unbent. Smollett has painted for us a brutal captain, and Marryat and Mitford have shown us a type which was, we trust, more common in the service. Some captains were, perhaps, the most cruel and tyrannical fiends ever permitted on the earth. There were never very many of this kind, but there were enough to make a number of our ships mere floating hells. They could single out and break the heart of any man whom they disliked. They could make life a misery to every man under them. They could goad a crew to mutiny, and then see them hanged at the yard-arm. It was a little thing to captains of this stamp to cut the flesh off a man's back with the cat-o'-nine tails, swearing placidly, as the poor fellow writhed at the gratings, that, "by God, he would show them who was captain, that he would see the man's backbone, by God." We know that other captains were respected and loved, and we read of ship's companies putting their shillings together to purchase silver plates, as keepsakes for such commanders, at the conclusion of a cruise. It must, however, be borne in mind that the sailors really preferred a man who was, in their terms, "a bit of a Tartar." They liked to sail with a smart and strict seaman who knew his duty, and made his men do theirs. They disliked slack captains as much as they disliked what they called "rogues," or tyrants. When a mild and forgiving captain came aboard a ship, either on a visit or to command her there was little interest displayed. But when a "rogue" or a "taut hand" came alongside there was a general rush to the ports to see the man.

The state of the ship, the happiness of her crew and the success of her voyage depended on the captain. In those days "every ship was a separate navy." Each captain had his own theories, and to some extent his own routine. He had also his own whims and fancies, with power sufficient to enforce them. Some captains took a delight in causing their crews to dress uniformly, in the slops supplied by the purser. Others took a great delight in inventing fancy uniforms for their coxswains and gigs' crews. A smart captain liked to dress his gig's crew in some distinctive dress—such as scarlet frocks, white hats, blue trousers, and black handkerchiefs; or white-and-blue guernseys, with white jackets and small-clothes. Some captains went to strange lengths to gratify their tastes. We read that the gig's crew of H.M.S. *Harlequin* were dressed up as harlequins, in parti-coloured clothes, to the great delight of the rest of the ship's company. We are also told of a gig's crew in kilts, with Scottish bonnets on their heads and worsted thistles on their jackets.

The captain's uniform varied a good deal during the forty-seven years of Nelson's life. At first it was a blue coat, with lace at the neck, blue lapels, white cuffs, and small flat gold buttons. A white-sleeved waistcoat, white knee-breeches, and white silk stockings completed the dress. The hat was a three-cornered black hat edged with gold lace, and bearing a cockade. At the time of Trafalgar, the lapels were white, the cuffs were striped with gold, the collar was stiff instead of drooping, and the waistcoat was no longer sleeved. A black cravat was worn about the throat. A straight dress-sword was worn, but its form was not prescribed by the regulations. The hat was the ordinary cocked hat worn athwartships. The hair was worn long, in a queue, tied with black silk ribbon. Powder or flour was used to dress this queue. It must be borne in mind that many captains wore pretty much what uniforms they pleased. Epaulettes came into use towards the end of the eighteenth century. They were of heavy gold stuff, hanging down in tassels from a central gold pad. Captains of over three years' rank wore them on both shoulders.

The lieutenant, "the officer next in power and rank to the captain," commanded in the captain's absence. A ship of the line carried from three to eight lieutenants, who took precedence according to the dates of their commissions. The first lieutenant was a sort of captain's proxy, who did all the work, in order that the captain might have the glory. He was responsible to the captain for the working of the ship, for the preservation of discipline, and for the navigation of the vessel from point to point, according to the captain's orders. He stood no watch at night when the ship was at sea, but he was expected to pass his days about the decks, and to come up in times of danger during the night watches. A lieutenant of the watch had to see that the helmsmen kept the ship to her course, that the log was duly hove every hour, and that the rate of sailing was marked on the board. He had to see that the men were alert and smart, at their proper stations, and ready for any sudden order. He had to keep the midshipmen and master's mates to their duty. He had to muster the watch, to keep the ship in her station, and to report strange sails and shifts of wind. He was to see that the look-out men at the mastheads and elsewhere were awake, and were not kept too long at their stations. If at night, in war time, a strange sail was sighted, he had orders to send a midshipman to the captain with the news. While the captain dressed he got the ship ready for action, keeping her out of gunshot of the stranger till all was ready. In the night he had to take particular care that the master-at-arms and corporals made their regular half-hourly rounds of all parts of the ship "to see that there is no disturbance among the men; that no candles nor lamps are burning, except those which are expressly allowed, and that no man is smoking tobacco in any other place than the galley." Twice in each watch a lieutenant had to send one of the carpenter's mates to sound the ship's well, and to see that the lower gun-deck ports were securely closed and barred. At the same time he had to send the gunner's mates to examine the lashings of each gun and to reeve double tackles or breechings if the guns were straining. In the morning he had to receive reports, from the boatswain as to the state of the rigging, and from the carpenter as to the state of the masts and yards. Any defects had to be reported to the captain. In addition to all these duties he had to keep an eye on the admiral's signals, to answer them directly his signalman reported them, and to record them carefully in the ship's log. At night, he had to see that lanterns were lit, and unshotted guns loaded, in case night signals had to be made. He had also to see that the cabin windows and other ports were closed so that the ship's lights might not be seen from a distance. In foggy weather he had to order the fog-signals, such as the firing of guns, beating on the drum, or striking of the ship's bell. He had to keep a log-book in the prescribed form, which volume he had to sign, and submit to the Navy Board, when he wished to receive his pay.

In action he commanded a battery of guns, and saw to it that the men kept at their quarters, and fought their guns with spirit. He had to take especial care that no loose powder was strewn about among the guns, and that the gun-captains took good aim at the enemy before firing. At all other times he had to "prevent all profane Swearing and abusive Language; all Disturbance, Noise, and Confusion."[1] He was to see that the men kept themselves clean "by washing themselves frequently," that the hammocks were often scrubbed, and the frocks and trousers washed. Junior lieutenants had charge of the ship's muskets, and exercised the seamen in musketry; for about 80 out of every 100 sailors had to be instructed in the use of the musket, to fit them for fighting ashore, should the service require it. In the absence of the captain, the lieutenant commanding might put an officer under arrest, or confine a man in irons, but he might not release nor punish any officer or man so confined, unless the captain were absent "with leave from the Admiralty" —*i.e.* for some considerable period, during which the lieutenant held his power. Lastly, the lieutenant had to keep all boats from coming alongside or leaving the ship without his express directions.

A lieutenant was often despatched on a press-gang to rout out the watermen and

---

1 *The lieutenant had perhaps improved in manners since Edward Thompson's time, when "a chaw of Tobacco, a ratan, and a rope of Oaths," were counted sufficient qualifications for a lieutenancy. Still, as many lieutenants were mates pressed out of merchant ships, there were many in H.M. ships who encouraged the chief faults mentioned in this article*

the sailors in the merchant vessels. "When the Ship has been sufficiently depopulated by ill-Usage," says Edward Ward, "my Spark is detached ashore, with some choice Hounds, to go hunt out a fresh Stock....he and his Bandogs together make a woeful Noise in all the Sea Port Towns round the Kingdom; he beats up all Quarters, and rummages all the Wapping Ale-houses, as narrowly as he would a Prize for the Indies. In fine, he's a perfect Hurricane in a little Town, and drives the laggard Dog along the Streets with as much Noise and Bustle, as Butchers do Swine at Smithfield."

The uniform of a lieutenant at the time of Trafalgar was as follows:—A coat of a rather bright blue, with white cuffs, white lapels, gold anchor-buttons, and long tails, was worn over a white cloth waistcoat, white knee-breeches, and white stockings. The sword was slung in a belt worn over the shoulder. The hat was a three-cornered black hat, with a cockade. It was generally worn athwartships.

Though this was the prescribed costume it was often departed from. Lord Dundonald mentions a first lieutenant, who received him on his joining the navy. He "was dressed in the garb of a seaman, with marline-spike slung round his neck, and a lump of grease in his hand, and was busily employed in setting up the rigging." Captain Glascock mentions another who "was dressed in a blue white-edged coat, which displayed here and there a few straggling anchor-buttons of different dies; to which was added a buff, soup-spotted vest, a pair of tarred nankeen trousers, and an old battered broad-brimmed leathern hat." This "homely habit" was splashed with pitch and whitewash. Michael Scott mentions another, as wearing a "curious wee hat with scarcely any brim," a worn old coat, "a dingy white Kerseymere waistcoat" and a pair of "ancient duck trousers."

Next in rank to the lieutenant, and in early days his superior, was the master. His chief duty was to "conduct the ship from port to port" under the direction of the captain. He controlled the sailing of the ship, the trimming and setting of her sails, and the guidance of her movements during a battle. He had, moreover, the charge of the stowage of the hold. He had to repair aboard his ship before she shipped her "iron and shingle" ballast, for it was one of his duties to see that the ballast put aboard was sweet and clean, and properly stowed. He had to superintend the shipping of the coals and firewood, and to note that a sufficient quantity was shipped to last the vessel for the period for which she was victualled. When provisions came on board he had to examine them to prove their soundness. He had to stow old provisions on the top, so that they might be eaten first. He had the care of the cable-tiers and spirit-room, and had strict orders not to allow a naked light to be carried into the latter place, lest the fumes of the rum and brandy should take fire. On no account whatsoever was he to quit the after hold while it was open. He had charge of the water-casks, but he was not allowed to pump out fresh water, for the use of the crew, without the captain's express commands. Every evening he had to examine all beer and water-casks, in order to report to the captain the quantity of water and beer remaining. He had to examine the cables to see that they were dry and clean, and clear for running. He had to keep the anchor clear when the ship rode to single anchor. He had to see that the standing rigging was well set up, and in good condition. He had to check the boatswain's and carpenter's accounts. He had to overhaul the sails in the sail-rooms to see that they were dry, in good order, not damaged by rats, etc.

Every day he had to find the ship's position, both by dead reckoning and by the altitude of celestial objects. When in foreign waters, near a coast, it was his duty to survey the inlets, from one of the ship's boats, keeping a most careful record of all soundings and bearings taken. He was to compare his own observations with those marked on the printed charts supplied to him. At noon, when he took the height of the sun, he had to call up his mates, with a proportion of midshipmen, with their quadrants, both to assist him and to teach them their business. He had to superintend the writing of the log book by his mates, who entered up all details of the weather, ship's position, expenditure of stores, and daily happenings, etc. etc., from the reports and records of the ship's officers. When the ship was in need of rope it was his duty to attend at the rope-walk to see the rope made, in order that the rope-maker should not waste his rope-yarns. Many masters sought to improve their pay by qualifying as pilots for some of the home and foreign ports.

First, second, and third rate ships carried what were known as second masters; while ships of all rates carried "master's mates" to assist the master in the dirtier parts of his business. These master's mates had to write up the log book, keep the fore yards trimmed, heave the log each hour, or half-hour, and keep the rates of the chronometers. They had also to attend in the hold when casks were being shifted. They were responsible for the discharge of various minor duties during their night-watches. In port they sent the midshipmen on periodical tours round the ship, "to attend to the hause," and to keep the men from lounging along the gun-decks. At night, at sea, they generally called the relieving lieutenant at the end of a watch. During the daytime a master's mate took charge of the lower-deck, and forbade "wrangling in the galley," or disorderly bawling about the waist, and the washing of clothes on days not set apart for that duty. He had to see that the cables and cable gear, were in good order; that the wash-deck buckets were in their places; and that sand-boxes or tin spittoons were always placed in the galley for the convenience of smokers. Another master's mate kept watch upon the main-deck to keep the deck as clear as possible, and to superintend all duty done in the waist. He had to keep the top-sail sheets clear for running, to attend the serving out of the beef, and the mixing of the wine and spirits.

A master's mate kept a record of the messes, for the assistance of the first lieutenant. He had to see to the numbering of the hammocks, the fixing of the hammock battens, the lashing and slinging of the hammocks, and the carrying of the scrubbed hammocks to the clothes lines on deck. He had to attend the "early dinner" at half-past eleven in the forenoon, when the helmsmen, sentries, and look-out men, who came on duty at twelve, had their food served out to them half-an-hour before the rest of the crew. Lastly, he was in command of the port-lids, and had to see them properly sloped, closed, or opened, according to the state of the weather; with the port-sills clear of sailor's property, such as hats or handkerchiefs.

A master's uniform was practically the same as the captain's, save that the lapels and cuffs were blue, instead of white. A master's mate wore a plain blue frock, with gold anchor buttons. The white knee-breeches, and white kerseymere waistcoats, were supposed to be worn by both ranks. Master's mates were often too poor to obey the strict letter of the regulation. They wore what clothes they had, and were not ashamed to purchase seamen's gear from the slop-chest.

Midshipmen, who were a step lower in the ship than master's mates, were generally taken aboard ships of war by the captains commanding. They owed their appointments to interest. The captains took them to oblige their relations, or in return for the cancelling of a tradesman's bill, or to curry favour with an influential family. As a rule, a midshipman was entered directly aboard the ship, as a "first-class volunteer," in which case he had to serve two years before he became full midshipman. But by passing two years at the Naval Academy at Gosport, the young man was enabled to ship as a midshipman on his first going to sea. In Nelson's time midshipmen sometimes began their sea-service at the age of eleven, or even younger. After 1812, no boy was borne on a ship's books until he was thirteen. An exception was admitted in favour of the sons of officers, who were allowed to be entered at the age of eleven. A first-rate ship carried 24 midshipmen; a second-rate, 18; a third-rate, 12; and fourth and fifth rates a proportionate number. The midshipmen of sixth-rates, and unrated vessels, were despised, and looked down upon, as a low lot, not to be recognised by those in crack ships.

Until the age of fifteen, the first-class volunteers, or midshipmen, were called "youngsters." They slung their hammocks in the gun-room, and messed, as a rule, by themselves, under the supervision of the gunner, who kept their clothes in order, and catered for them. In frigates it would seem as though they went at once to the steerage, to mess with their seniors. Those of them who were not perfect in their navigation, nautical astronomy, and trigonometry, were taught, every forenoon from nine till twelve, by a duly certificated schoolmaster, who drilled them very carefully in the sea-arts and sciences. The schoolmaster was expected to reprove and repress the slightest immoral tendency his pupils displayed. He had also strict orders to report the idle and vicious to the captain. The schoolmaster was nearly always the ship's chaplain, who received £5 from every midshipman he instructed. In those ships which carried neither schoolmaster nor chaplain the captain himself taught the youngsters, and made them bring up their quadrants to take the sun at each noon; and refused to let them sup until they had worked out "the ship's position" by dead reckoning or the altitude of the sun. When the school hours were over, and the ship's position found, the youngsters were sent on deck, in their respective watches, to learn their duty. They were looked upon as the slaves of the first lieutenant, who generally used them as messengers. They were usually employed on boat service, and sent to and fro in the ship's boats when the ship was in port. When at sea they had to mix much with the men in order to learn their duty. They were expected to keep order when the men were at the braces or aloft, or at general quarters, and to report those who were idle, noisy or absent. They had to stand their watch at night like the lieutenant, but as the officers were divided into three watches, which had eight hours below to every four hours on deck, this was not a very terrible hardship. They had to see the hammocks stowed in the morning, and to report those sailors whose hammocks were badly lashed. They had strict orders not to lounge against the guns or ship's sides. They were not allowed to walk the deck with their hands in their pockets. Some captains made the midshipmen responsible for the working of the mizzen-mast, and sent them aloft to furl the mizzen-royal and mizzen-topgallant-sail whenever sail was shortened. The midshipmen were expected to go aloft with the men to learn how to furl or reef a sail, how to bend and unbend canvas, how to set up rigging, and all the other arts of seamanship. Midshipmen were always stationed in each top when sails were being furled, in order to cheer up the men to a lively performance of their duty. Other duties given to them were the supervision of the hoisting in of stores; the command of watering parties; mustering the men at night; watching the stowing or cleaning of the hammocks—and generally fetching and carrying for their commander and tyrant the first lieutenant. In the night-watches they had to keep awake upon the quarter-deck, "to heave the log and mark the board," and to be ready to run any errand for the officer of the watch.

When they had reached the age of fifteen, and had been duly rated as midshipmen, they became "oldsters," with increased pay, freedom from the schoolmaster, and an allowance of grog. At this stage they shifted from the gun-room into the midshipmen's berth on the orlop deck, in the after cockpit, where they messed with the past midshipmen (who had qualified as lieutenants and awaited promotion) and with the master's mates. After another two years they were qualified to take the examination for masters mates, provided they had perfected themselves in navigation and in seamanship. At the age of nineteen, if they could prove that they had had six years of sea service, they were allowed to go before the Navy Office examiners (or a quorum of three sea-captains) to be examined as to their fitness for the post of lieutenant. It was not essential that they should first have passed the examination for master's mate, but many midshipmen took this preliminary step, as it qualified them to navigate prizes into port.

The pay of a midshipman varied in the different rates. Aboard a first-rate, he received £2, 15s. 6d. a month; aboard a third-rate, £2, 8s.; and aboard a sixth-rate, a bare £2. A first-class volunteer received £9 a year, from which £5 were deducted for the schoolmaster. It was essential that a first-class volunteer or midshipman should have private means. For a volunteer some £30 or £40 per annum was considered sufficient. For a midshipman the necessary annual sum ranged from £70 to £100 according to the station on which his ship served. Foreign stations, owing to the ruinous exchange, were more expensive than the Channel or the Mediterranean. The sum, whatever it was, was paid in advance to the captain's agent, particularly in the case of the youngsters, so that the captain was able to check extravagance among the boys, and to keep them from "vice and idleness," when the ship was in port.

A midshipman wore a dirk or hanger, when in uniform. His working coat was cut short, like the round blue jacket of a man-of-war's man. His uniform was a blue tailcoat lined with white silk. It was of good blue cloth, ornamented with small gold anchor-buttons, and with a white patch on the collar, known as a turn back, or a "weekly account." His breeches and waistcoats were of thin jean or white nankeen. His hat was three-cornered, high and smart, with a gold loop and a cockade. For foul weather he had a glazed hat. Round his neck he wore a black silk handkerchief. His shoes were black. His shirts were of frilled white linen. In heavy weather he wore a frieze overall, known as a watch-coat, and waistcoats of scarlet kersey-mere. This was the ideal, or prospectus, midshipman, of the sort the poor child imagined before he came up the ship's side. There were other kinds.

After a long absence from port, when the lad's clothes were worn out or stolen, or "borrowed," he had to purchase clothes from the slop-chest or go in rags. The boys seem to have been treated with the utmost laxity. In many ships they were allowed to be slovenly. We read of a midshipman coming on to the quarter-deck with only one stocking, with a dirty shirt, torn coat, and wisps of straw in his shoes. For the rough sea service this attire was quite fine enough, and a down-at-heel appearance was not reckoned disgraceful. When asked to dine with his captain, the mid. took greater pains with his appearance, and borrowed from all who would lend, in order to appear neat. In battle, and when at sea, he wore his oldest and dirtiest rags. For boat service he was required to dress with greater nicety, in order that the honour of the ship might be maintained among the shore-goers.

A midshipman's mess was not a pleasant place. It was generally below the water, in the after cockpit, in a dingy den, lit partly by a lantern, and partly by a thick glass scuttle, crusted with filth, let into the ship's side. From deck to beam it measured, perhaps, 5 feet 6 inches, so that its inhabitants had to uncover as they entered it to avoid crushing their hats against the ceiling. Twelve feet square was reckoned fairly large for a berth. Any berth big enough for a fight when the chests had been cleared away was looked upon as roomy. The atmosphere so far below water and the upper air was foul and noisome. The bilges reeked beneath the orlop in a continual pestilential stench, unlike any other smell in the world. Near the berth, as a sort of pendant to the bilges, was the purser's store-room where the rancid butter and putrid cheese were served out once or twice a week to the ship's company. Farther forward were the cable-tiers, with the tarry, musty smell of old rope always lingering over them. In many ships a windsail or ventilator led from the deck to the berth to relieve the midshipmen with a little fresh air.

There was not much furniture in the midshipmen's mess. Nearly all had a table, not from any generosity of the Government, but because the table was wanted for the surgeons in their operations after battle. This table, at meal-times, was covered with a cloth or old hammock, which had to last a week. The cloth was used at meal-times as a dish-cloth and knife-and-fork cleaner. At meals the table was lit by tallow dips or purser's glims, stuck in beer or blacking bottles. After meals, and for state occasions, "the green cloth," a strip of dirty baize, was substituted. For seats the "young gentlemen" used their chests. There was no decoration on the walls or bulkheads of a berth. Nails hung with clothing, quadrants, boxing gloves, single-sticks, hangers, etc.

etc., were the only decorations ever known there. Some berths may have had lockers to contain their gear, bread-barge, table utensils, and sea-stores. Some may have had a tank to hold the allowance of fresh water. The berth was kept clean by a mess-boy, a dirty, greasy lad, unfit for anything else. This worthy washed the weekly table-cloth, and saw to the cooking. All midshipmen were blessed with other servants, known as "hammock men." These were either old sailors or marines, who compounded to lash and stow, and carry down and unlash, the "young gentleman's" hammock for the sum of a glass of grog, payable each Saturday night. For further considerations of grog or tobacco the hammock man sometimes washed the young gentleman's shirts while the ship was at sea. In port, the linen went ashore to some reputable, or disreputable, washerwoman, who was lucky indeed if she saw the colour of her money.

The berth was the home of the elder midshipmen, the master's mates, the captain's clerk, and, at times, the assistant surgeons. As some of the midshipmen, in nearly all ships, were nearer forty than twenty, and as many of the master's mates were grey-headed men, the berth was not the place for little boys, especially when the rum was flowing towards 8 p.m. The elders seem to have understood as much, for they had a custom of sticking a fork in the table, or in the beams above it, directly the first watch was set. As soon as the fork was in its place every youngster and youth at once retired to his hammock, so that the old grizzled veterans had the board to themselves. Probably they were good-hearted fellows in the main, if a little rough from the life, and a little soured by their long and unrewarded service. But, if one or two writers may be trusted, their conversation was not well calculated to improve the mind. Indeed, in one or two ships, the veterans had a rule that no one should join their nightly rum-drinkings till he had passed an examination in vice. Youngsters who disregarded the signal of the fork were given a few minutes' grace, after which the signal was repeated. If "the geese" remained "in the berth" after the second signal, they were colted (or whipped with a knotted cord) and flicked with twisted handkerchiefs till they scattered out to their hammocks.

The food served out to the young gentlemen was the same as that issued to the men. The King's provisions were generally supplemented by little niceties, purchased in port by the caterer of the mess. This worthy was usually a master's mate of some authority in the berth. Each member of the mess paid him from £3 to £5 on joining the ship, and about £1 a month while the ship was in commission. The caterer expended this money as he thought fit. Before leaving England he used to lay in a great supply of potatoes and onions, which he stowed in the lockers, or under the table, or in strings dangling from the beams. Dutch cheeses, for the manufacture of a midshipman's luxury called "crab," were also purchased, together with tea and coffee and small stores, such as pepper and sugar. In port the caterer purchased "soft Tommy" (or shore bread) and boxes of red-herrings. The ship's allowance of spirits was so very liberal that it was not necessary to add to it. A pint of navy rum a day was sufficient, or should have been sufficient, for any man.

Captain Chamier, Captain Maryat, Jack Mitford, Captain Sinclair, Captain Glascock,

Augustus Broadhead, and the author of "The Navy at Home," have all painted vivid pictures of the life in the midshipmen's berth. It was rough and ready, and sufficiently brutal. There was a good deal of noisy horseplay, a good deal of vice and cruelty, and a little fun and sea philosophy, to allay its many miseries. A midshipman lived on "monkey's allowance—more kicks than halfpence," and had to put up with bullying and injustice unless he was strong enough to hold his own. A weakling was robbed of his fair allowance of food, and imposed upon in other ways, as by tardy relief at night, after keeping his watch on deck, etc. A thin-skinned or sensitive boy was out of his element in such a place. There was no privacy aboard a man-of-war. A student or scholar had little opportunity for reading. Down in the berth, during the daytime, there was a continual Dover Court ("all talkers and no hearers") so that study there was out of the question. A midshipman was continually fighting, quarrelling, or playing the fool. The berth was a sort of bear-garden, a kind of "sea-Alsatia," which not even the captain would control or keep in order. From the central darkness of the steerage many cutting out expeditions were organised against the captain's steward or the purser, or anyone with anything eatable or drinkable. The berth was always the noisiest and most lawless place aboard. With fiddling, singing, shouting, and fighting[1] the mid. passed his leisure. He was careless of all things save his dinner and his sleep. As for his duty one has but to consult the authorities to see how he regarded that.

According to Lord Cochrane's lieutenant there was no "such a thing as a faultless midshipman." According to others the breed thought of nothing but gormandising, and were so greedy that "though God might turn their hearts, the very devil could not turn their stomachs." The young gentlemen were seldom out of hot water. The usual punishment inflicted on them was mast-heading, by which a lad was sent to the top-mast, or topgallant cross-trees, for several hours at a time. This punishment was often the cause of the loss of a meal, for no member of the berth thought of the absent one at dinner. In some cases a mid. was mast-headed for a full twenty-four hours, during which time he had to depend on the topmen for his meat and drink, if he failed to steal down privily to lay in a stock. The punishment of mast-heading in sunny latitudes was not very severe. Most midshipmen used to look upon it as a pleasant relaxation. They could lash themselves to the cross-trees and fall asleep there during daylight in fine weather, while at night they could creep down unobserved to the top, to take a nap on the studding-sails, after telling the topmen to answer for them if hailed from the deck. Some lieutenants took a shorter way with midshipmen. They would lash or "spread-

1   *"Twas folly trying*
to read i' th' Berth—for what with shying
Hats about—and playing flutes,
Backgammon—Boxing—Cleaning Boots,
And other such polite pursuits.
Skylarking—Eating—Singing—Swigging,
And Arguments about the Rigging,
'This Mast how taut!' 'That sail how square'
All Study had been fruitless there."
        Thus Jack Mitford from his gravel pit in Battersea

Plate 3(a) There is little visual evidence of what a gun-deck in action looked like but this working model at the Victory Museum in Portsmouth gives an idea of the hell it was. (b) A marine stands guard, ready to shoot those who failed to carry out orders in battle.

Plate 4 *(a) The worm, used to scour out any burning scraps which might remain in the gun after firing. (b) The sponge, pushed through the barrel after the worm. The rope handle saved the sailor from leaning out too far and exposing himself to enemy sharpshooters. (c) Powder horn, used by the captain of the gun to prime the gun powder charge through the touch hole. The priming was ignited either by slow-match or flint-lock.*

eagle" the offender in the weather rigging, some half-a-dozen ratlines above the hammock nettings. In this position, with his face to windward, and his arms and legs widely stretched, the midshipman cooled in the wind for an hour at a time, with the spray sprinkling him at brief intervals. This was severe punishment, usually given for sleeping while on watch. Another punishment for the same offence was dowsing, or drenching the offender with a bucketful of water poured from a height. This was known as "gram-pussing," or "making him a soused gurnet." Some captains even went so far as to order the boatswain's mate to rig a grating in the cabin, and to lay the offending midshipman either on that grating or on a convenient gun, and to give him a dozen with a colt, or knotted rope's end. Jack Mitford mentions a case of this sort, and a case occurred on the Australian station in the early forties. In the latter case the offending captain was court-martialled, and severely reprimanded, "which was nuts to every midshipman in the service."

The midshipman's berth was governed partly by the strong arm and partly by certain laws designed to give an air of justice to the cruelty they recommended. Any member of the mess caught eating, or drinking rum, in the berth, on the day on which he dined in the cabin or ward-room, was sentenced to be firked or cobbed with a stockingful of sand, a knotted rope, or a cask's bung stave. In extreme cases "faulty relief," by which a lad was kept on deck after his watch was out, was punished in the same way. Anyone caught taking an unfair share of the rum was firked or cobbed, provided that he was not too big a man to tackle.

As for amusements, one did not come to sea for pleasure. It is significant that the chief amusement or game in use in the midshipmen's berth, was "able whackets," a pastime in which cards, blasphemy, and hard knocks were agreeably mingled. Other amusements they had none, save that old one, mentioned by Cervantes, of laughing at sea-sick persons. A green hand, or Johnny Newcome, was fair sport for his first few days aboard, but tying knots in a lad's sheets, or putting a slippery hitch upon his hammock lanyard, or stowing round shot and swabs under his blankets, soon failed to amuse the jokers. Cutting a man down as he slept; hiding his trousers in the oven in the galley; sending him to the top to gather gooseberries or to hear the dog-fish bark, or to get the key of the keelson, or to find Cheeks the marine—all of these little tricks were jests of the sea humourist, designed to sharpen the wits of the greenhorn. Borrowing a new chum's clothes was a more questionable piece of humour, for the lender seldom saw his gear again, unless he had sufficient strength to back his claim. Making a new-comer drunk on navy rum and sending him on deck, with a message to the officer of the watch, was yet another jest. There were one or two others, which we will forbear to mention.

A midshipman was expected to "turn out" of his hammock at half-past seven every morning. If he hesitated, and lingered on the order, and turned, like the sluggard, instead of showing a leg, he was very promptly cut down and hauled from his blankets by main force. When he had turned out he washed himself in a little tin basin, balanced on the lid of his chest. He was allowed to wash every day, unless the supply of fresh water was running short. He then dressed, and blacked his boots, and cleared up his sleeping quarters, so that the breakfast table should not be littered with blacking brushes, soap, or wet towels. At eight he took his breakfast of tea and biscuit, or cocoa and porridge. At nine he went to the schoolmaster.

Although many midshipmen were mere children they had "extraordinary privileges, which they abused extraordinarily." They were officers, and therefore powerful. A midshipman had power to bully and maltreat all those beneath him. Aboard H.M.S. *Revenge,* just before Trafalgar, under a captain so strict and just as Robert Moorsom, there was a midshipman who amused himself by climbing on to gun-carriages, and calling to him the strongest and finest of the sailors. It was this little devil's pleasure to kick and beat the poor fellows without cause. He was an officer, and to resent his cruelty would have been mutiny. A midshipman had but to complain to a lieutenant to get a man a flogging at the gangway. He had full leave and licence to curse and misname any seaman who displeased him. It was in his power to follow a man day after day, visiting him with every oppression that malice could suggest. The seaman had no remedy. Appealing to Caesar, the captain, was worse than useless. The man had to grin and bear it, and count himself lucky if he escaped the cat-o'-nine-tails. "By the god of war," said Sir Peter Parker to his seamen, "by the god of war, I'll make you touch your hats to a midshipman's coat, if it's only hung on a broomstick to dry." There was no redress to be gained from men holding opinions of that kind.

Chapter IV

The civilian and warrant or standing officers / The surgeon /
the surgeon's assistants / The chaplain / The boatswain / The
purser / The gunner / The carpenter / Mates and yeomen /
The sailmaker / The ship's police / The ship's cook

The surgeon, who messed with the ward-room officers, and slept in a cabin near the ward-room, had to pass an examination at the Transport Board, in addition to that imposed by Surgeon's Hall, before he could receive his warrant. He was "generally the most independent officer in the ship," as his duties were essentially different to those of the executive. He had charge of the sick and hurt seamen, of the medicines and medical comforts, and of the ship's hygiene generally. On coming aboard a ship commissioning he had to examine the doctor's stores, and to see them duly stowed away in the medicine-chests or sea-dispensary below-decks. When the newly raised or pressed men were brought aboard he had to sound them and examine them, not only for their fitness for the service, but for any trace of infectious or contagious disease. When the "quota men," or my Lord Mayor's men, came before him he caused hot water to be prepared, so that the men could have their heads shaved, and their bodies scrubbed "from clue to earring," and their clothes very zealously boiled before they mixed with the crew. At sea he had charge of the sick-berth, or sick-bay, a small sea-hospital shut away from the rest of the ship by wooden screens covered with canvas. As a rule this sick-bay was in the forecastle, on the starboard side, but sometimes circumstances made it necessary to pitch it on the orlop-deck, out of the way of the enemy's shot. Any sailor who felt sick reported himself to the surgeon, or his assistants, in the forenoon. If he was found to be ill he was removed from duty, and sent into the sick-bay, where a certain number of the "waisters," or least necessary of the crew, acted as nurses to him. These sick-bay attendants kept the place scrupulously clean, well fumigated, and sprinkled with vinegar.

A surgeon's most common duty at sea was the dressing of ulcers, to which the seamen were very subject. In Smollett's time the assistant-surgeon had to repair daily, in the forenoon, to the space about the foremast, where his loblolly-boy, or dresser, banged a mortar with a pestle, as a signal to the men to repair on deck to have their sores dressed. In ships newly commissioned, typhus, gaol, or ship fever was very common. The surgeons, as we have seen, did all they could to prevent it, by disinfecting the quota men, and by boiling or burning all "cloathes" brought from "Newgate, or other suspected Prisons." In spite of all they could do the gaol fever destroyed large numbers of sailors every year. At sea the most dreaded complaint was the scurvy.

Surgeons had standing orders to examine all those seamen who appeared in the least dejected or sickly. The sailors disliked the sick-berth, and always hesitated to report themselves when ill, because those in the sick-bay had to go without their grog and tobacco. The lieutenants sometimes helped the surgeons to pick out a sickly man before his ailment had fully declared itself. By these means the epidemical complaints were kept under. If a surgeon detected the least trace of scurvy in a man he had to see that the fellow received a daily dosing with lime-juice, a drink then newly instituted as an anti-scorbutic. Some ships which had no lime juice used essence of malt, or molasses, or raw potatoes, for this purpose.

A surgeon was expected to have a number of dressings always prepared, in case the ship should "be suddenly brought to action." He was also expected to instruct the crew in the use of the tourniquet, so that men with shattered stumps might have some chance of living until the surgeon could take up their arteries. He was to visit sick and wounded men twice daily, to see that the sick-bay stove, of "clear-burning cinders," was kept alight, and to make a careful record not only of the sick men treated, but of the means taken to prevent infection. A wooden ship, built of wood improperly seasoned, was always damp and foul, "tending to produce disease and generate infection." The ballast was often dirty; the water in the bilges was always putrid; the hold and orlop were badly ventilated; and the gun-deck was packed like a sardine tin with several hundreds of men, not all of whom were even tolerably cleanly in their habits. It was a surgeon's duty to ask the captain to fix a general washing-day once in each week, whenever there was plenty of rain water, so that the men's clothes might be washed and then dried in the sun. At intervals he was to ask that all the hammocks should be aired on the forecastle, the lashings taken off, the blankets shaken, and the mattresses hung in the sun. Now and then he had to fumigate the ship. The most common means of doing this was by burning a preparation of gunpowder, soaked in vinegar, in iron pans about the decks. The powder sputtered for a long time, sending out a quantity of acrid smoke, which was reckoned a powerful disinfectant. Burning flowers of sulphur gave good results, and many found fires of fir wood satisfactory. In dock, when a ship was very badly infected, they seem to have used tobacco, burning it in great pans about the gun-decks, with the ports and hatches closed, and the men standing at their quarters "as long as they can bear it." Sometimes the seamen's kit bags were hung up over "pots of burning brimstone." Sometimes pots of burning brimstone were placed between the guns and sprinkled with vinegar. A very wholesome practice was the immersion of red-hot irons, called loggerheads into buckets of tar. This last method was generally used to disinfect the sick-berth, when there were many sick. A surgeon was expected to ask the captain from time to time to cause iron fire buckets, containing burning charcoal, to be lowered into the hold. The red embers were sprinkled with vinegar and brimstone as soon as the buckets were in position. The well, the bilges, and the recesses of the hold, were thus both dried and disinfected at the same time. Another way of fumigation was by pouring sulphuric acid and the powder of nitre upon heated sand. After Nelson's death this was the plan generally adopted.

In spite of all the fumigations the ships were never free from unpleasant smells: the dank fusty smell of dry-rot, the acrid and awful smell of bilge water, and the smells of decaying stores and long defunct rats. Windsails and canvas ventilators were always fitted, in fine weather, to drive pure air into the recesses; but fine weather is the exception, not the rule, to the north of the fortieth parallel. The ships were sometimes battened down for days together, till every inch of timber dripped with salt water and the condensation of the breaths of many men. One who knew these old ships has testified that "there was always more or less stench" aboard the best regulated ship, but that the stench was less penetrating, and the danger of infection always slighter, in those ships which were frequently dried by portable fires. A diligent surgeon, if he had the fortune to sail with a sensible captain, could do much to better the condition of the entire ship's compnay.

The sick and wounded men were treated with comparative humanity. They were given nightcaps, hair mattresses, free vaccination, and sheets of real linen. The cook was sometimes bidden to boil up some "sowens," or "flummery," from the ship's oatmeal for them. The very sick were given soft bread and "portable soup." When fish were "caught for the ship's company," they got the first helping. When the officers had any fowls or similar delicacies in the ward-room, they often sent portions forward for the sick-bay, with any wine they had. But there were, nevertheless, certain cruel regulations in force which made the lot of some of the sick men sufficiently terrible. Lint was reckoned too expensive to be used for the washing of wounds. Sponges were used instead, but the supply of sponges was limited, and, in action, one sponge was often used to dress the wounds of a dozen men. This practice naturally favoured the spreading of various common forms of blood-poisoning. A man with a slight cut or abrasion ran a very good chance of losing a limb by the poison of an infected sponge. Another most barbarous restriction limited the supply of mercury, as "being requisite only for complaints that might be avoided." A man attacked by one of those complaints was not allowed to leave his duty, he was mulcted more than two weeks' pay for the medicines he drew, and no care was taken to separate him from his uninfected shipmates.

At the beating of the drum to quarters, the surgeon and his assistants were expected to repair to the after cockpit, to fit it for the reception of the wounded. Some of the non-combatants, such as the purser, the stewards, the chaplain, and the captain's clerk, accompanied them, to help the wounded men according to their power. The midshipmen's chests were drawn together, into a kind of platform. A sail was strewn over the top of them in several folds, as a sort of couch for the maimed men. In those ships in which the midshipmen were without a table the chests were used for the operation-table, though they were too low for comfortable surgery. When the operating table had been cleared, some large candles were placed upon it, in tin sconces, to give light to the surgeons. Other candles, in heavy ship's lanterns, were arranged about the bulkheads. A portable stove was lighted, for the heating of oils, etc., during the operations. A kid of water was generally heated there, in which the surgeons could warm their saws and knives before commencing amputations. They did this, not as a modern surgeon would

41

do it, to sterilise the steel, but in order to prevent the torture caused by the coldness of the metal against the raw flesh and bone. At the sides of the table were ranged several kids or half-tubs, some of them empty, to receive amputated limbs, some of them full of water for the washing of the surgeon's arms, or for the cleansing of wounds. Close to the operating table were some opened bottles of spirits for the refreshment of those very weak from pain and loss of blood. There were also full supplies of styptics, bandages, sponges, tourniquets, saws, knives, etc. etc., all ready to hand, under a good light.

Before the firing began, the surgeon and his assistants stripped to their shirts, rolled up their sleeves to the shoulders, and braced themselves for a very ghastly experience. A few minutes after the fighting commenced, the wounded came down, supported or carried by their shipmates, who laid them on the operating table, and on the platform prepared for them. A few minutes firing at close range would generally send a dozen or twenty wounded men to the surgeons. It was the strict, inviolable rule, that a wounded man should take his turn. The first brought down was the first dressed. No favour was shown to any man, were he officer or swabber. The rule was equitable, but not without its disadvantages. Many men were so torn with shot or splinter that they bled to death upon the sail long before the surgeon worked his way round to them. The sailors were indeed taught the use of the tourniquet, but it is one thing to adjust a tourniquet on a mate's arm, at the word of command in a quiet drill hour, and quite another to fix it upon a stump of raw flesh that is pumping blood, in all the fury and confusion of a sea-fight. Not many of the men brought down to the surgeons were properly bandaged.

A ship's cockpit during a battle must have presented a lively picture of hell. There was the long narrow space shut in and cramped by the overhead beams and lit by the evilly smelling tallow candles. Up and down the deck in rows were the wounded, on their bloodstained sail. Every now and then some heavy feet padded down the hatchway, announcing the advent of another sufferer. Up above was the thundering of the leaping and banging cannon, which roared irregularly, shaking the ship in every timber. Nearer at hand were the poor wounded men, some of them stunned, and chewing placidly; others whimpering and moaning, some screaming and damning. Up and down the rows went the chaplain and civilians, with weak wine-and-water, lime juice, etc., for those in need of drink. In the centre of the piece, bent over the table, were the operators, hard at work. There was no time for lengthy diagnosis. The wound was always self-evident, red, and horrible. Its extent and seriousness had to be guessed from a glance. The surgeon's first act was to rip off the bloody clothes with his scissors, to bare the wound. A single hurried look had to suffice. From that look he had to determine whether to amputate or to save the limb, whether the wound were mortal or worth dressing, etc. etc. If he decided to amputate, he passed his ligatures as a man would take turns with a hammock-lashing. The assistant gave the patient a gulp of rum, and thrust a leather gag into his mouth, for him to bite upon in the agony of the operation. After that, it took but a moment to make the two cuts, and to apply the saw, while one assistant held the patient's body, and another the limb or fragment of

42

limb which was coming off. There was really no time for delay. Men were perhaps bleeding to death at every second, and it behoved the surgeons to hurry with each case.

The assistant-surgeon was generally a young man fresh from Surgeons' Hall. He was expected to keep a record of all cases brought before him, to visit the sick in the sick-bay, and to do his best to cheer them. He dressed the men's ulcers every forenoon, and had control of the slighter general cases. A first-rate ship carried three assistants; other large ships, two; and the smallest, one. An assistant surgeon sometimes accompanied wooding and watering parties, particularly in those places where the men were likely to be long ashore. It was his duty on these expeditions to look after the health of the men, to keep them from drinking putrid water, and eating acid fruits in the heat of the day. In tropical climates he dosed them religiously, twice every day, with a heavy dose of "bark" in a glass of wine.

Neither the surgeon, nor his assistants, wore uniform until the beginning of 1805. The pay varied with the length of service. A surgeon who had served twenty years, received 18s. a day. One who had served six years received 11s. a day. The assistants had to serve three years before they ranked as full surgeons. There were three grades of assistant surgeons, and the regulations enforced a year of service in each grade. The pay of the lowest grade was 4s. a day. The other two grades received 5s. a day. Both surgeon and assistants were expected to supply their own instruments.[1] Their medicine and other gear were supplied by the Government. When not employed aboard the King's ships, or in the King's naval hospitals, the surgeons and assistants drew half-pay.

The chaplain of a ship of war (he was generally known as the rook, the psalm-singer, or the sky-pilot) had to be a clergyman of the Established Church. Many ships carried a chaplain, for the Admiralty instructions compelled them to accept any properly recommended clergyman "of good moral character," who cared to offer himself for the berth. It is not certain what position chaplains held in the ships of Nelson's time, but they probably had cabins "in the ward-room or gun-room," and ranked and messed with the ward-room officers. They received a stipend of about £150 per annum, with an extra allowance for a servant, and a bounty of £20 a year to all who qualified as school-masters at the Trinity House. The captain had orders to see that the chaplain received "every proper attention and respect, due to his sacred office." He had also to order the ship's company to hear divine service and a sermon every Sunday morning, "if the duties of the ship, or the state of the weather do not absolutely prevent it." He had, moreover, to use his influence to support the chaplain, by preventing "all profane cursing and swearing, all drunkenness, gaming rioting and quarrelling, and in general everything which may tend to the disparagement of religion, or to the promoting of vice and immorality." The chaplain, for his part, was expected to take care of the midshipmen, and to teach the ship's boys (or cause them to be taught) their catechisms and the Holy Scriptures. The boys who said their catechism well were rewarded with sixpences. Those who were idle or stupid were punished. The chaplain had to attend

---

1 *We believe that this was not always properly done. We read of the wounded in one ship being operated upon by a saw from the carpenter's stock. A stiff upper lip was very necessary aboard a ship of that kind.*

the sick and wounded in the sick-bay or cockpit, "to prepare them for death, and to comfort or admonish them." Those who died at sea were buried by him at the gangway in the presence of all hands. Those who were killed in action were generally thrown overboard without service of any kind. In some ships, even as late as the battle of the Nile, it was the custom for the ship's company to muster to prayers before going into battle. In times of stress, in storm, when the ship was on fire, or sinking, etc. etc., the chaplain was to set an example of Christian fortitude, and to cheer the men to their duty while the danger lasted. Captain Glascock tells a tale of a chaplain aboard the *Moeander,* who took his spell at the pumps to encourage the seamen. Marryat tells of another, who helped to put out a fire.

Some ships carried a schoolmaster in addition to the chaplain. It was the duty of the schoolmaster to teach the young gentlemen the art of navigation for two or three hours each morning. A schoolmaster received from £2, 8s. to £2 a month, with a bounty of £5 for each midshipman in his class. He messed with the ward-room or gun-room men, wore plain or civilian clothes, and slept in a cabin near the ward-room, or in the steerage. To receive an appointment as schoolmaster one had to pass an examination in navigation before the authorities at Trinity House.

Next in importance to the second masters, and ranking above the master's mates and midshipmen, was the boatswain, an officer, indeed, but a warrant or standing officer, not "on the quarter-deck," like the gentlemen we have been describing. A boatswain had charge of the "boats, sails, rigging, colours, anchors, cables and cordage." He was generally an old sailor, grizzled and tanned, who knew his business as well as it could be known. No man could be appointed boatswain until he had served a year as a petty officer, to the satisfaction of his captain. On receiving his warrant he was expected to get his stores on board, and to examine every inch of rigging in the ship, in order to test its soundness, before the ship sailed. When at sea he was expected to make such an examination daily. On going into action he had to see that the chains, etc., for repairing the rigging, were in their places. He had to keep an eye upon the sailmaker, and to see that the sails in the sail locker were properly stowed, and kept dry. He was one of those officers honoured with "all night in." He worked on deck at the discharge of his duty, from sunrise to sunset. He slept at night either in his cabin in the fore cockpit or in a favoured place upon the lower-deck, where double the usual swinging space was allowed for his hammock. He had a distinctive uniform, of blue cloth, with blue lapels and collar, white or blue trousers according to taste, and gold anchor-buttons on the coat, cuffs, and pockets. His hat was the usual glazed, low top-hat, with a cockade on one side. He wore linen shirts or woollen jerseys just as he pleased. About his neck hung a thin silver chain, supporting a silver whistle— the badge of his office. When an officer gave an order the boatswain sounded the call peculiar to that order down the hatchway, while the boatswain's mates, his assistants, repeated it, till the ship rang with the noise. Directly the order had been given, the boatswain and his mates slipped down the hatchways, and hurried the crew to their duty with their colts and rattans. A boatswain always carried a cane, the end of which was waxed and "tip'd with simple twine-thread." He had the power to thrash the laggards, and to cut at those who did not haul with sufficient fervour when the men were at the ropes. "This small stick of his," says Edward Ward, "has wonderful virtue in it, and seems little inferior to the rod of Moses, of miraculous Memory; it has cured more of the Scurvy than the Doctor, and made many a poor Cripple take up his Bed, and walk; sometimes it makes the Lame to skip, and run up the Shrouds like a Monkey." The boatswain's cane and the colts of his mates continued to do execution till after 1815, when they were gradually laid aside. The privilege of the cane was very much abused. It encouraged the warrant officer to treat his subordinates cruelly, and the lives of those subordinates were made sufficiently miserable as it was.

In action the boatswain was stationed on the forecastle, which he commanded. At all times the boatswain had to see that clothes, etc., were not hung up to dry in the rigging. He had to take care that the ship's fresh water was not diverted for the washing of the seamen's clothes or hammocks. He had to keep the yards square when in port, and at all times he had orders to prevent ropes or lines from trailing overboard. Once a day, in fine weather, he was expected to lower a boat and row round the ship, to see that her outward trim was satisfactory, and that nothing needed to be repaired. In the mornings, when the hands were turned up, he had to go below with his mates to see the berth-deck cleared of hammocks. Laggards and sluggards who did not turn out, or hurry their hammocks away, were then enlivened by the colt or the cane. Those whose hammocks were not lashed up and stowed by eight bells, or 8 a.m., were reported to the officer of the watch. Their hammocks were taken from them, and locked up for a month in the boatswain's store-room. The sluggard had to pass that month without a hammock as best he could, sleeping under the guns, or on deck, or in the tops, in considerable misery. Slighter punishments were meted out to those who did not number their hammocks so that they could be readily identified. The boatswain took his meals in his cabin in the fore cock-pit. He had a ship's boy to wait upon him, or, at least, shared a boy with the carpenter. In a home port, when the ship was laid up "in ordinary" (i.e. not in commission), the boatswain remained on board, with his mates and yeomen, and a few other standing officers, to help the dockyard men in their dismantling or rerigging of the vessel. While "in ordinary" the boatswain stood watch at night, to prevent desertion, or fire, etc., and to keep away shore boats bringing contraband (such as drink) to the men on board. His pay varied from about £4, 16s. a month in a first-rate to about £3 a month in a sixth-rate. His assistants—the ropemaker, yeomen, and boatswain's mates—received from two guineas to two guineas and a half a month. One of the last of the boatswain's privileges or duties was that of "piping the side" when a captain came aboard. Lastly, he had charge of the boats when they lay in-board on the booms. One of the boats, either the yawl or the long boat, was under his care at all times, just as the captain's gig or dinghy was always in charge of the coxswain.

The boatswain's mates, his immediate subordinates, were chosen from the very best seamen on board. They were the leaders or drivers of the crew, and generally the finest men in the fleet. They wore no uniform, but the pay they received, being £2, 5s. 6d. a month, enabled them to wear neater clothes than the seamen. They had the unpleasant duty of flogging misdemeanants at the gangway. They slept in favoured places on the lower-decks, with rather more space for their hammocks than was allowed for a seaman. The boatswain's yeoman, who kept the boatswain's stores in order, generally slept in the wings, near their post on the orlop-deck.

Ranking with the boatswain as a standing or warrant officer, and drawing exactly the same pay, was the purser—the officer in charge of the ship's provisions. A purser, like a boatswain, received his warrant direct from the Admiralty, but the fore-mast man had no chance of becoming purser without friends and influence. A purser was not usually promoted to his post for merit. He was generally a friend of the captain, one of the captain's "followers" or servants, going with him from ship to ship, and feathering his nest very handsomely from every cruise. A purser could not receive his warrant till he had served a year or eighteen months as a captain's clerk, or keeper of the ship's books. The captain usually appointed his own clerk, or at anyrate recommended his own choice for the appointment. He had therefore considerable power over his purser, and often shared the plunder that worthy gathered. Before a man could commence duty as a purser he had to sign a bond, giving "two proper and competent persons as his securities." The "penal sum" mentioned in this bond varied considerably, according to the size of the ship. The purser of a first-rate had to find securities for £1200; for a third-rate, £800; and for a sixth-rate, £400. This regulation made it impossible for a man without influence to obtain a purser's place. Very often it led to grave abuses, for it frequently happened that the guarantors came forward with their securities merely to get the purser into their clutches. As a purser's sureties were generally merchants, it followed that the purser was frequently squeezed into buying their goods, at their prices, to the prejudice of the poor sailors. In many cases the purser bought his place as captain's clerk, by bribing both the captain and the Admiralty officials to give him the appointment. When he had qualified himself he bought his warrant as purser in the same way, trusting to his own dishonesty to recoup himself.

A purser had to see that the ship received her full quantity of water, spirits, and provisions. He was expected to examine the meat and bread, to make sure that all was sound, and stowed in sound casks. He was to have the key of the purser's store or steward-room, on the orlop-deck. Twice a day, if the captain gave the order, he had to open this room, to serve out provisions to the cooks of the messes, weighing every atom with scrupulous care. The times of serving out were generally from seven to nine in the morning, and from six to eight in the evening. To encourage him to be careful and thrifty he received a bonus on the provisions remaining with him at the end of a cruise, when the ship was paid off. He also received 10 per cent. on all sums paid to the crew "for savings of provisions." He was allowed a certain sum for the waste of casks, sacks, and iron hoops, but he was expected to pay for all deficiencies in excess of that sum. He had to provide the ship with "coals, firewood, turnery-ware, candles, lanterns, etc," out of a sum known as Necessary Money, which the Government allowed to him. He received, in addition to the Necessary Money, an annual allowance "upon passing his account"—a sort of Government reward for probity. This reward in a first-rate ship amounted to £25.

A purser was expected to exert himself to save the public money as much as he could. Old and bad meat, which had been in salt for a few years, was often issued to him in new casks, with new marks upon them. A purser had to see that this old meat was issued before the new salt meat was broken open. "The purser," says the regulation, "is to issue out first such part thereof as he shall have perceived most liable to decay." His most important duty was the keeping of the ship's muster book, a lengthy folio, in which the name of every person "belonging to, or borne on the books of, the ship," was carefully entered, with some short description of the man, to enable the runners to trace him if he deserted. The entire crew were mustered from this book every tenth day while at sea, and immediately after every action. Any man who was absent without leave for three successive musters was marked with an R, for run—i.e. deserted. A man so marked lost all the pay due to him. The book marked the date of all discharges from the service, with the cause of such discharge, "whether it be death, desertion, or otherwise." In addition to the muster book a purser had to keep very careful and minute accounts of the expenditure of the provisions. If the supplies ran short he had to superintend the purchase of a fresh stock, if there were no "instrument of the Victualling Office" at the port where the ship refitted.

A most important duty allotted to the purser was the keeping of the slop books. "Slops" were the sailor's clothes and sea-bedding, supplied by the naval storekeeper to every ship in commission. The slops were placed in the slop-room on the orlop-deck in the care of the purser. Seamen and pressed men who came aboard destitute were allowed to purchase from the slop-room to the amount of two months' pay. After this first purchase they were allowed to spend 7s. a month in slops if they could show that they really needed them. No man was allowed to buy slops until he had received a written permission from his lieutenant. Seamen in rags, or in want of bedding, could be forced to purchase slops, to the amounts just mentioned, so that no man appeared disreputable as long as the slops held out. As the gear supplied from the slop-room was of uniform pattern, the crews of the ships were generally dressed alike. The slops usually carried were white canvas kit-bags, scarlet marine tunics, blue coats, waistcoats, and trousers, checkered blue-and-white shirts, black silk wrappers, Dutch, fur and worsted caps, straw mattresses, blue or brown blankets, thick woollen stockings, heavy weather trousers, and the usual seaman's frocks and shoes. As the shoes usually worn were low, the slop-room generally contained a supply of silver buckles for those seamen who liked to be neat. The purser who had charge of the slops at sea received a shilling in the pound on all sales, from the contractor who sent the goods to the navy store-keeper. A similar sum was paid to him on the sales of dead men's effects, which were sold by auction on deck directly the man had died. No man was allowed to bid at these auctions unless he could prove that he was in real need.

The dishonesty of pursers has long been proverbial. There may have been honest

47

pursers, but they were in the minority. They were usually rapacious sharks, who bought their places, and made hay while the sun shone. Their robberies and knaveries affected the sailors more than the Government. The sailors had no redress, and the Government system was so faulty that the frauds were never brought to light. A purser had many ways of making himself rich at the expense of the poor tar. At the time of which we write he was probably a less open thief than his forerunners in peculation—the pursers of Queen Anne and the later Stuarts—but he was no less clever in turning a dishonest penny. A very favourite way of making money was the old way of adulterating the ship's wine, or giving vinegar in lieu of wine.[1] "He oft-times turns Water into Wine, and Wine into Water, with one mere Fiat to his Steward." Another most lucrative way was that of getting a man "lent" to another ship, or sent ashore, thereby forfeiting his wages. When a man had been sent out of a ship in this way the purser neglected to strike his name off the books. When the ship was paid off the purser would forge a pay-ticket for the amount due to the poor fellow, and draw the whole sum. The slops were always sold at more than their value, so that the amount of the commission might be more handsome. Slops were also sold to dead men, and charged upon the dead men's wages. The purser drew his commission on the sale, and kept the slops so sold. It was often said that a purser could make a dead man chew tobacco. He could also make a corpse buy clothes, and drink his allowance of grog. By restricting the supplies of firewood, and of the vile tallow dips or candles, a purser was often able to make something out of his Necessary Money. In those ships in which he was in league with the captain he found it possible to keep live stock, such as hogs or cattle, on the oatmeal charged to dead sailors.

A purser's uniform was exactly the same as that of a boatswain. Being usually of more gentle breeding than a boatswain, he wore a three-cornered cocked hat, instead of the glazed, sailor's top-hat. He also wore white knee-breeches and white stockings, instead of trousers. In action, he either retired to his berth below the water-line, out of danger of the shot, or went to the cockpit to moisten the lips of the wounded with weak rum-and-water or lime juice. In some ships he was placed in command of the powder passers, a line of men engaged in handing cartridge boxes from the magazines to the gun-deck. In those ships to which the naval storekeepers sent Bibles and prayer-books it was the duty of the purser to distribute the books to the ship's company, under the direction of the chaplain. After December 1798 the ships were supplied with tobacco by the Victualling Board. The purser had charge of the tobacco during the cruise, and received a commission on all he sold, with a small "allowance for wastage." He was not allowed to sell more than 2lbs. of tobacco in the month to any man, nor might he charge more than 1s. 7d. a pound for the commodity. A purser's steward (the creature appointed to assist a purser) seems to have received about 35s. a month for his services, with the privileges of standing no watch and sleeping on the orlop-deck.

Ranking with the boatswain and purser, as a standing or warrant officer, was the

---

1 *Money was advanced to the purser for the purchase of wine. He generally bought weak, or adulterated wine, at a low price, and pocketed the money saved.*

48

gunner, the officer appointed to take charge of the ordnance and ammunition. He was generally appointed after twelve months' service as a petty officer, if he could pass a *viva voce* examination in the art of gunnery. His first duty on getting aboard a ship fitting for the sea was to place the gun carriages at their respective ports, and to superintend the reeving of the breechings and side-tackles. He was assisted in this duty by a little gang of men placed under his orders, and known as the gunner's mates and gunner's crew. When the guns came on board from the storekeeper he had to examine them and see them mounted in their carriages. He had next to examine the magazines, to test them for damp, to clean them, and to see them hung with felt. He was to prove the locks on the magazine padlocks, and to make sure that a set of felt or soft leather slippers was always hanging near the hatch, for use by all folk entering the magazine. When the ship took aboard her powder it was his duty to see all lights extinguished throughout the ship, save the lanterns in the light-rooms which lit the powder-magazines. He had to lock the magazines when the powder was shipped, and deliver the keys to the captain. At sea he had to examine the ship's guns, and to see that they were ready for action. He had to take care that each gun was fitted with crows, sponges, etc., and that the "cheeses," or nets of gun wads, were ready beside each gun carriage. He had also to see that the shot racks running down the ship's sides along the waterways and round the coamings of all the hatches were filled with scraped and hammered shot. He had also to prepare a quantity of "match," and to keep it ready for use in the match tubs, and to see that none of it was burnt during the day, and that "two lengths" of it were kept alight at night over tubs of water. He had to see the tops supplied with powder and hand-grenades. He had to keep his canvas grape-shot bags exposed to the sun and wind, so that the canvas might not moulder. He had to receive the stores issued for the use of the armourer, and to superintend that official in his cleaning and scouring of the muskets and small-arms. He had to keep the gun-tackle blocks well greased, so that they might work easily. He had to turn his powder barrels end for end from time to time, to prevent the separation of the nitre from the other ingredients. He was to fill a supply of cartridges for immediate use. In battle he was to make use of any lull in the firing to keep this supply undiminished. Before an action he had to hang up wetted frieze blankets round the hatchways leading to the magazines. He had also to go the round of the gun-decks, to make sure that every gun was ready for action. From time to time, in fine weather, the gunner was to air his stores, under a marine sentry, on the upper-deck. At all times he was to examine the guns and their fittings at least once a day, and to report their condition to the lieutenant. He was also expected to instruct the "people"—i.e. the ship's company—in gunnery, a duty which he sometimes neglected. He slept and messed with the junior midshipmen in the gun-room. He had one servant, one ship's boy, allotted to him, to wait upon him, while his store-rooms, etc., were kept clean by his mates or crew or "yeomen." He stood no watch at night, but worked all day from "turn out" till the setting of the watch. His uniform was the same as that of the purser and boatswain, a white-lined blue coat, with blue lapels and cuffs, white kerseymere breeches or trousers, and gold anchor-buttons on the pocket flaps. His pay was the same as that given to the boatswain and purser, but he received in addition a small perquisite, the sum of one shilling being paid to him for every powder tub returned in good condition to the storehouse. The pay of his subordinates—the gunner's mates yeomen of the powder-room, and quarter-gunners (i.e. men in charge of four guns each)—varied from about £2, 2s. to £1, 16s. a month. These lesser dignitaries wore no distinctive uniform, but they had various little privileges—such as snug corners for their sleeping quarters on the berth-deck, or in the cable tiers, etc.

Of greater importance than the gunner and boatswain, and sometimes drawing more money for his services, was the carpenter, or "wooden artist." No man could aspire to be a ship's carpenter till he had faithfully served his indentures with a shipwright, and been a voyage to sea as a carpenter's mate. To get an appointment a carpenter had to pass an examination at Shipwrights' Hall before a quorum of master shipwrights. A ship's carpenter had to know his trade. He could not get his place by jobbery or influence. On getting aboard a ship he was expected to examine her with great care and to report any defective timbers, and to have them removed. He had to keep the pumps in good order, and the boats ready for launching. He was to go aloft every day, to examine the state of the masts and yards, particularly after heavy weather. He was to keep the ventilator rigged whenever the weather was sufficiently fair. He was to sound the well each day, and to take care that it never contained more than 15 inches, and that those 15 inches were frequently changed, lest the water should putrify. He was to have a variety of shot plugs prepared, of different sizes and varying material—as lead, oakum, felt, rolled rope, canvas, etc. In battle he was to walk along the orlop-deck with his mates to repair any shot holes as they were made. At sunset each night he had to report to the first lieutenant that his stores, such as shot-plugs, axes, etc., were ready for action, and that the masts and spars were in good order. He had to take especial care that the decks and topsides were kept well caulked, lest water should leak in and drip from deck to deck, to the misery of all hands. To enable him to do all these duties properly he was granted an assistant, in large ships two assistants, known as the carpenter's mate or mates. These men received two and a half guineas a month, and slung their hammocks in favourable places on the lower gun-deck. In addition to the mates, all ships above the fourth-rate carried an officer called the caulker, who likewise drew two guineas and a half a month. This officer was directly under the carpenter, and had standing orders to search out and caulk all defective seams in the deck and topsides. In addition to the duties indicated above, a carpenter was always to see that the port-lids were in good trim. In foul weather it was his duty to close those on the lower-deck, and to make them watertight with oakum. While at sea he had the power to discharge, or cause to be discharged, any caulker or carpenter's mate not worth his salt. His subordinates were always stationed on the main-yard in furling sails. As a rule, they stood no night watch, but were expected to come on deck for any important duty, such as tacking ship, shortening sail, sending down spars, etc.

A carpenter's pay aboard a first-rate ship was £5, 16s. a month. Aboard a third-rate he drew about £1 a month less. In fourth, fifth, and sixth rates, he drew exactly the same pay as the boatswain, gunner, and purser. He slept in his cabin in the fore cockpit, or in some den in the steerage. He had a boy to wait on him, or shared one with the boatswain. In fine weather he rigged his carpenter's shop on the second or upper gun-deck, in the clear, well-lit space between the tiers of guns. In foul weather his work was done below, in his workshop in the fore cockpit.

Ranking with the boatswain's mates, in first and second rates, were the quartermasters, the assistants of the master, and master's mates. The quartermaster was a petty officer, drawing £2, 5s. 6d. a month for his services. He was generally an old and trusty seaman, who was not sufficiently active to be employed as a boatswain's mate. His duties were to superintend the helmsman; to assist in the stowage of provisions or ballast; to coil away the cables in the cable-tiers; to keep the time, and to cause the ship's bell to be struck at each half-hour. When the purser served out provisions in the morning and evening a quartermaster always attended, to watch the weighing, etc. He wore no distinctive uniform, but he had the privilege of sleeping below the berth-deck, in the cable-tiers, on the orlop-deck.

The sailmaker, who drew the same pay as the quartermaster, received his appointment by warrant from the Navy Office. He was helped by a mate or assistant, drawing some 7s. a month less money, and by a "crew" of two men, who were clever with needle and palm. His duty was to keep the sails in good repair, and in order, so that they could be readily brought on deck from the sail-room in the orlop or hold. In fine weather he worked on the second or upper gun-deck, repairing old sails, putting in patches or new roping, etc. He stood no watch, and slept in a favoured place, abreast of the fore hatchway on the lower-deck.

The chief of the ship's police, the man responsible, under the first lieutenant, for the preservation of peace and quietness below-decks, was the master-at-arms. At the end of the eighteenth century he had lost much of his old authority, and his ancient duty of instructing the seamen in the use of the musket was usually performed by the junior lieutenant. A master-at-arms was appointed by a warrant from the Board of Admiralty. His pay varied from £2, 15s. 6d. in a first-rate to £2, 0s. 6d. in a sixth-rate. When at sea he sometimes drilled the sailors in the use of the musket, and had special orders to see that they took good aim before firing. His chief duty was to keep a strict lookout for unauthorised lights or fires, extinguishing all lights and fires at the setting of the watch, and reporting all those who presumed to re-light them. He had to walk round the ship at intervals, to make sure that no purser's glim was burning in any of the store-rooms, or in the cable-tiers. He had to prevent any smoking outside the galley, and he had to report any person found using a naked candle below-decks. These duties were comparatively harmless. They saved the ship from being burnt, while at no time did they interfere much with the comfort of the ship's company. Even the restriction of the smokers to the narrow space of the galley, where but few bluejackets could take tobacco at a time, was not reckoned a hardship. Smoking was not so popular at that time. Comparatively few men smoked. Nearly all of those who used tobacco chewed it, "like Christians." But the master-at-arms made himself very objectionable in another way. He was the head of the ship's police, continually on the lookout for the petty criminal. He passed his days ferreting out the privy drunkards, the quarrelsome, riotous, gambling, and sportive persons, so that the captain might punish them at the gangway with a couple of dozen. When a man or woman came on board from the shore it was the duty of the master-at-arms to examine him (or her), to annex any spirits which might be concealed in the person's clothes. When a boat came alongside he had to report that she contained no intoxicants, before her lading was allowed to be hoisted in-board. Any man found drunk, or fighting, or playing at cards, or dicing, or using a candle, or otherwise transgressing the iron laws of the fleet, was promptly arrested by the master-at-arms, and placed in irons, and chained to an iron bar by the mainmast, till the captain could judge and sentence him. At evening muster, the master-at-arms stood in a prominent position, to spy out any man who walked a shade unsteadily or answered to his name with a thick intonation. He was armed with a cane, with which he was entitled to deal out punishment to those whom he suspected of playing the spy upon him. Those who wanted a little quiet fuddle in between the guns, or wished to play a game of cards, or to dice each other for their tots of grog, would send out spies, and post sentinels, to warn them of this officer's approach. To checkmate these outposts the master-at-arms encouraged the meaner sort to act as his "narkers," or informers, to let him know when, and by whom, and where, unlawful pleasures were being enjoyed. These police spies, or ship's traitors, were known as white mice. They lived uneasy lives aboard a man-of-war. Sometimes the crew fell upon them privily, and man-handled them. A master-at-arms was not altogether safe. In the dark night-watches, as he made the round of the lower-deck, with his lantern in his hand, those whom he had caused to be flogged would sometimes get revenged.

In all those ships which did not carry marines a master-at-arms was expected to post sentinels, and to instruct them in their duty. He was assisted in his work by two or more satellites, known as ship's corporals, who received about two guineas a month a-piece. One or more of these officers was continually walking about the ship after the setting of the watch at 8 p.m. They stood their watches, like the rest of the crew, but they had the privilege of sleeping near the ship's side, with rather more space than their shipmates. In the daytime they pried up and down in search of delinquents, whom they might thrash with their rattans or drag to the bilboes. They were appointed to their positions for merit, but he who made the appointment saw to it that the men promoted to these particular posts were naturally fitted for them. The job was not popular among the sailors, for the increase of pay was slight, the responsibility heavy, and the duty unpleasant.

An important member of the ship's crew was the cook. This warrant officer was appointed by the Commissioners of the Navy, who invariably chose him from the Greenwich pensioners. He was seldom blessed with all his limbs, and never rose beyond the making of pea-soup and the boiling of junk. "The composing of a minc'd Pye," says Edward Ward, "is metaphysics to him." He did not cook for the captain. His art was of the popular kind. Anyone could understand it. There was nothing intense or

Cabin-boy

Sailor

Carpenter

Purser

Midshipman

Captain of Marines

Lieutenant

Captain

Admiral

POLL OF PLYMOUTH'S PRAYER.

CHARMING THETIS, thou who bluſheſt not at ſleeping with the Sun, a Buxom Nymph addreſſes thee, from the ſign of the Punch-Bowl: aid, I beſeech thee, her endeavours to pleaſe the gallant protectors of our ſea-girt iſle, and haſten the return of the homeward-bound Eaſt-India fleet, may it be richly laden, and may I partake of the ſpoils. Steer, I pray thee, the whole crew into our harbour, and grant that not a man may forget his Polly, who ſickens with deſpair, till ſhe ſees the gay ſtreamers floating in the wind. Guard, I entreat thee, from danger, my favourite *Jack Oakem*, do not forget *Tom Splice*, and my beloved *Bob Stern*, neither withdraw thy favours from *Ben Bobſtay*, *Harry Hawſer*, and many more that I could mention; they are all generous fellows, and bleed freely, as to *Dick Junk*, he is a wary ſee gull, but having his will in my power, thou mayeſt do with him as beſt pleaſes thy wiſdom.

Thou knoweſt I have ſix heavy ſilver watches, four large coral necklaces, and other trinkets, at Mr. Gripe's the Pawn-Broker's, enable me, I pray thee, to redeem them, that I may appear lovely in the eyes of the whole fleet. Grant me but theſe favours, and thy name ſhall be remembered by myſelf, and the jolly Tars of England, in Bowls of Punch, large as the capacious ocean!!

SPRAGG, PRINTER, 27, BOW-STREET, COVENT-GARDEN.

Plate 6 *Poll of Plymouth's Prayer.*

mysterious about it. His duty was very simple. He had to steep the salt junk served out to him in a barrel of salt water, known as a steep tub. When the meat had become a little soft and pliable, through the dissolution of the salt, he took it and boiled it for several hours, or until the boatswain piped to dinner. It was then served out to the different messes. Directly the last piece had been handed out the coppers were skimmed. The salt fat or slush, the cook's perquisite,[1] was scraped out and placed in the slush tub. The coppers were then scoured, and made ready for the cooking of the next meal. A cook was not allowed to give his slush or melted fat to the men, as they used it in making their private duffs or puddings, and "scarcely anything more unwholesome, or more likely to produce the scurvy, can be eaten." A cook was expected to be frugal with his firewood, except after a battle, when he had generally a stack of splinters to eke out his store. He was expected to keep his galley clean, and usually had a mate or assistant, with the full complement of limbs, to help him in this work. His pay was very small, being only about thirty-five shillings a month, but as he was always a Greenwich pensioner, in receipt of 11s. 8d. a month relief, and as he generally cleared a handsome sum from his slush, the pay was sufficient. He wore no uniform, kept no watch, seldom strayed very far from his galley, and slept at nights on the lower gun-deck, in a favoured place, with a ship's corporal for his neighbour. The marines kept guard at the galley door while he cooked the dinner, lest the ship's thieves should privily convey away his delicacies while his back was turned. He was expected to extinguish his fire after the meal of the day had been cooked, and at all times when the ship prepared to go into action. In port he was expected to keep a poker heated for the firing of salutes, etc. At sea, he was allowed to cook little messes for those of the hands who were his cronies. In some ships he was also allowed to dry the clothes of those wetted by the sea in heavy weather. His coppers were examined every morning, by the mate of the watch, before the "cocoa," or "oatmeal," was put into them.

1 *Half of all the slush went to the cook. The other half went to the ship, for the greasing of the running rigging.*

Chapter V

The people / The boys / Manning / The divisions / The messes
The dress / The King's allowance / Grog / Marines

There were various ways of entering the Royal Navy, "through the hawse-holes." The greater number of our seamen were pressed into the fleets from merchant-ships, or sent aboard by my Lord Mayor, or by the sheriffs of the different counties. A large number volunteered in order to get the bounty. But a certain percentage joined the fleet as boys, either through the Marine Society, or from love of adventure. The Marine Society sent a number of lads to sea in each year. Their boys were generally between thirteen and fifteen years of age. Some of them were "recommended" by magistrates for petty crime or vagrancy. Some were beggars, or street Arabs, snatching their living from the gutters. Some were errand-boys, horse-holders, shop-lads, etc. Most of them were poor children, whose parents could not clothe nor feed them. Some were apprentices, or charity boys, who were more "inclined to hazard their necks than to live a sedentary life." The Marine Society gave these lads a brief preliminary training aboard a ship in the Thames, under a boatswain and boatswain's mate. They then sent them to sea, in men-of-war, as ship's boys or volunteers of the second and third classes. As ship's boys, they received £7 or £8 a year, which kept them in clothing till they were strong enough to rank as seamen. A ship's boy was generally put to all the dirty and trivial work of the ship, such as cleansing the pig-stys, hen-coops, head, etc. A number of them were rated as servants to the midshipmen, boatswains, warrant, gun-room and ward-room officers. These wretched creatures lived the lives of dogs, particularly those allotted to the midshipmen. Those who were not made servants were hunted about and bullied by the sailors, who loved "to find the opportunity to act the superior over someone." Those who survived the brutality of their shipmates, and failed to desert from the service, in time became ordinary seamen, drawing 25s. a month.

A boy was allowed half the usual ship's allowance of rum and wine. He received pay for the half he did not draw. With the ration allowed to him—half-a-gill of rum, and a quarter of a pint of wine a day—he was able to get blind drunk, or to purchase little luxuries, just as he pleased. If he got drunk, or in any other way transgressed the rules of the navy, he was flogged, but with the boatswain's cane instead of with the cat. In action, he was stationed at a gun, with orders to supply that gun with cartridges from the magazine. He was not allowed to supply more than one gun with powder until the boys of some of the guns were killed or wounded. In a hot engagement he was kept running to and fro, over the bloody and splinter-scattered deck, carrying the cartridges from the magazine. He was warned to carry his cartridges under his coat, so as to avoid the flying sparks from the touch-holes. If he tried to bolt away from the magazine into the shelter of the orlop-deck the midshipman stationed at the hatchway promptly shot him, or beat him back with the pistol butt. The boys (with good reason) were generally berthed apart from the men. They seem to have slung their hammocks in the sheet-anchor cable-tiers, or on one of the upper gun-decks, according to the size of the ship in which they sailed.

The true man-of-war's man, or bluejacket, was said to have been "begotten in the galley and born under a gun." He was a prodigy, "with every hair a rope-yarn, every tooth a marline-spike, every finger a fish-hook, and his blood right good Stockhollum tar." This kind of man-of-war's man was rare. When he sailed aboard our men-of-war he generally held some position of authority, as captain of a top, or boatswain's mate. We had never a ship's crew of his like, even at the beginning of the French wars, when our ships were manned by the pick of the merchant-service. There were other kinds of sailor, for the King was always in want of men, and a man-of-war refused nothing.

The Royal fleets were manned, as we have seen, by various expedients. A certain proportion of the man-of-war's men came to sea as boys, and remained in the service all their lives, partly because they were too strictly kept to escape, and partly because "once a sailor always a sailor"—the life unfitted them for anything else. A large number joined the navy because their heads had been turned by patriotic cant; and very bitterly they repented their folly after a week aboard. A number came willingly, from merchant-ships, attracted by the high bounties or premiums, offered for seamen volunteering. Some came willingly, deceived by those placards in the seaports, which promised abundance of grog and plenty of prize-money to all who entered. But the greater number came unwillingly, by the imprest or quota, or from my Lord Mayor. The press-gang was especially active in securing sailors from merchant-vessels. Very frequently they stripped such ships of their crews and officers, leaving their captains without enough hands to work the ships home. It was a cruel hardship to the poor merchant-sailors; for often, on coming to a home port, after a long voyage, they would be snatched away before they had drawn their wages. Instead of enjoying a pleasant spell ashore they would be hurried aboard a King's ship, to all the miseries of a gun-deck. It was the custom to say that a sailor was better situated on a man-of-war than on a merchant-vessel; that he had better food, better treatment, and better money. As a matter of fact the merchant-seamen regarded the Royal Navy with dread and loathing. There can be little doubt that the thought of the press-gangs, and the fear of service in the navy, drove many of our best merchant-seamen into American ships, where they were rather less subject to impressment. In the war of 1812 a number of them fought against, and often helped to defeat, the English frigates and small men-of-war.

We live at a convenient distance from those times, and regard them as glorious.— "The iniquity of oblivion blindly scattereth her poppy." Man is always ready to ignore the pounds of misery and squalor which go to make each pennyweight of glory. Our

55

naval glory was built up by the blood and agony of thousands of barbarously maltreated men. It cannot be too strongly insisted on that sea life, in the late eighteenth century, in our navy, was brutalising, cruel, and horrible; a kind of life now happily gone for ever; a kind of life which no man to-day would think good enough for a criminal. There was barbarous discipline, bad pay, bad food, bad hours of work, bad company,[1] bad prospects. There was no going ashore till the ship was paid off, or till a peace was declared. The pay was small at the best of times, but by the time it reached the sailor it had often shrunken to a half or third of the original sum. The sailor was bled by the purser for slops and tobacco; by the surgeon for ointment and pills; and by the Jew who cashed his pay-ticket. The service might have been made more popular by the granting of a little leave, so that the sailors could go ashore to spend their money. It was the long, monotonous imprisonment aboard which made the hateful life so intolerable. When the long-suffering sailors rose in revolt at Spithead, they asked, not that the cat might be abolished, but that they might go ashore after a cruise to sea, and that they might receive a little more consideration from those whose existence they guaranteed.

Having secured a number of reliable sailors from the merchant-ships and sailor's taverns, the captains of men-of-war commissioning filled up their complements by taking any men they could get. The press-gangs brought in a number of wretches found in the streets after dusk. It did not matter whether they were married men with families, tradesmen with businesses, or young men studying for professions: all was fish that came into the press-gang's net. The men were roughly seized—often, indeed they were torn from their wives by main force, and knocked on the head for resisting—and so conveyed on board, whether subject to impressment or not. They could count themselves lucky if their neighbours came to the rescue before the press-gang carried them off. When once they were aboard they were little likely to get away again, for though they had permission to "state the case," if they thought themselves illegally seized, the letters of appeal were very seldom successful. The press-gangs were sometimes rewarded with head money to make them zealous in their duty.

We have already described the Lord Mayor's men. We will now describe the "quota." or "quota-bounty" men, such as manned our fleets from 1795-1797. It was found that neither the press nor the bounty attracted men in sufficient numbers. Laws were passed by which the English counties were compelled to furnish a quota of men according to an established scale. The English seaports were put under a similar contribution. The sheriffs of the counties, and the mayors of the seaport towns, at first found the arrangement by no means a bad one. They were able to ship off their rogues, criminals, poachers, gipsies, etc., without difficulty. After a time, when the rogues had grown wary, they found it difficult to make up the quotas. They had to offer bounties to

1 *"In a man-of-war," says Edward Thompson, "you have the collected filths of jails; condemned criminals have the alternative of hanging or entering on board..... There's not a vice committed on shore that is not practised here; the scenes of horror and infamy on board a man-of-war are so many and so great that I think they must rather disgust a good mind than allure it."*

induce men to come forward; bounties in some cases amounting to more than £70. It was said of the "most filthy creatures" who took advantage of the bounties that "they cost the King a guinea a pound." They came aboard coated with filth, crawling with parasites, "so truly wretched, and unlike men," that the lieutenants must have been disgusted to receive them. Criminals sentenced at the sessions were offered the alternative of going to sea. The direct consequences were that our ships of war were frequently manned by criminals and petty thieves, who stole from each other, and skulked their work, and deserted when they could. The lower gun-decks became the scene of nearly every vice and crime in the calendar. Theft aboard ship was punished with cruel severity, but these shore-going gentry robbed right and left, in gangs or singly, as though their fingers were indeed fish-hooks. Dr Johnson was right in wondering why folk came to sea while there were gaols ashore. Perhaps no place has contained more vice, wickedness, and misery, within such a narrow compass, than a ship of the line at the end of the eighteenth century.

When a ship's crew[1] had been brought aboard they were examined by the first lieutenant, who lost no time in allotting them to their stations. Elderly, reliable seamen, who knew their duty and could be rated as able, were stationed on the forecastle to do duty about the anchors, bowsprit, and fore yard. They were called sheet-anchor or forecastle men, and next to the gunner's crew and boatswain's mates they were the finest men in the ship. They took great pride in making the forecastle the cleanest and trimmest place aboard. A visitor anxious to learn the state of the discipline of a vessel had but to go forward to her forecastle. If the forecastle were spotless, the hammocks well stowed, the paint work and bright work brilliant, and the ropes pointed and beautifully flemished, then the ship (he might be quite sure) was in pretty taut order. A forecastle or sheet-anchor man slept on the lower deck, far forward.

Having picked his forecastle men, a lieutenant had to select his "topmen." There were three divisions of topmen, one for each mast—fore, main, and mizzen. The topmen had to work the three masts above the lower yards. The lieutenant chose for the topmen all the young, active seamen who had been to sea for three or four years. Their work was very arduous, and very exacting. It was the hardest work of the ship, and demanded the smartest men, yet no men were more bullied than those to whom the duty fell. A topman lived in continual terror. He was at all times under the eye of the officer of the watch. His days were passed in an agony of apprehension lest something should go wrong aloft to bring him to the gangway. Smartness aloft was, to many captains, the one thing essential aboard a man-of-war. A topman had to be smart, and more than smart. He had to fly up aloft at the order, lay out on the yard, reef or furl, lay in, and be down on deck again, before a boatswain's mate could draw his colt. The sailors raced "mast against mast" whenever sail was made or shortened, and whenever a spar was struck or sent aloft. They were not only smart, they were acrobatic. They were

1 *The pay of an able seaman, such as a topman or forecastle hand, was 33s. a month. An ordinary seaman received 25s. 6d. The landsman 2s. 6d. or 3s. a month less. Until 1797 the pay given was about a third of that quoted above.*

known to run aloft and to run along the yards to the yard-arms, and this in blowing weather, and with the ship rolling. But, no matter how swift they were, the captain and lieutenant, who watched from the deck, wished them to be swifter. It did not matter to these two flinty ones whether the men were doing their best, and breaking their hearts to do better. All they cared for was the honour of the ship, and perhaps a word from the admiral. Then it was:

"What are you doing on the yard, there? Are you all asleep there, mizzentop? The main-topmen are nearly off the yard. Stow that bunt, you crawling caterpillars, or I'll stop the grog of the lot of you."

Then the curses and blaspheming followed, with threats of the cat and disrating. The poor fellows on the yard would redouble their efforts, dripping with sweat as they pounded the heavy canvas into the skin. That was the heart-breaking part of the business: doing one's level best and getting damned for one's pains. Then, directly the job was done, a wild rush from the yard took place. Many captains had the savagery to flog the last man down, so that every man risked his neck to get down quickly. In reefing top-sails this rule invariably punished the best man—i.e. the man at the yard-arm or post of honour. The captains do not seem to have considered that the last man down was generally the first man up. Their cruelty caused the death of many poor seamen, who fell from aloft while racing up or down, or while working recklessly on the yard. An old sailor has told us of a captain of a top who deliberately threw himself overboard rather than suffer punishment for some slight irregularity aloft. "These men are frequently punished," says Jack Nastyface, "and are always in dread when aloft lest they should be found fault with for not being quick enough, for punishment is sure to follow, and sure enough their conjectures are too true: for they are not only flogged, but their grog is stopped."

Next in importance to the topmen were the men of the after-guard, a company composed of poor seamen and landsmen, despised by all the real sailors. The duties of the after guard were easy, if dishonourable. They worked the after braces, the spanker, main-sail, and lower stay-sails. It was their duty to keep the after parts of the ship clean. At quarters they were stationed at guns on the gun-deck, or as sail-trimmers, or as small-arm men, as the lieutenant directed. The after-guard in a first-rate ship numbered about 90 men, while the forecastle, fore and main tops were manned by from 60 to 70 each. A mizzentop needed fewer men, from 25 to 30 being the usual number. The after-guards, marines, and waisters invariably manned the capstans when anchor was weighed.

The largest division of a ship's company, and the most ignoble, was that of the waisters, the men stationed in the waist, the men "without art or judgment," who hauled aft the fore and main sheets, and kept the decks white. They were the scavengers, swabbers, pumpers, the doers of the ship's dirty work, the pigsty keepers, and ship's sewer men. They were sometimes ordinary seamen who were strong enough but too stupid to be stationed aloft. Generally they were landsmen, unfit for other duties. They had charge of all the live stock, if the ship carried any, and he that was "good for nothing else" was "good enough for a waiter." Large ships generally carried about twice as many waisters as after-guard men. In small ships the proportion was more nearly equal.

Lastly, there were the idlers, or men with day duty, who stood no watch at sea. Among these were the holders, who lived in the hold, in perpetual semi-darkness, creeping about, on their queer occasions, among the casks and stinks. Then there were the poulterers, who fed the captain's geese in the boats on the booms, or crammed the chickens in the hen-coops. Then there were painters, in charge of the port-red, yard-blacking, side-yellow, and white, with the oil for mixing them and the brushes for laying them on. There were tailors, who made fine clothes for the crew of the captain's jolly-boat, and did odd jobs, for payment, for the other members of the crew. There were the mast men, one to each mast, to keep the ropes beautifully coiled, and the brass on the fife-rails polished. There were butchers to kill the live stock and fatten the pigs; barbers to clip and shave; and hairdressers to dress the men's queues, and comb out the wigs of the officers. There was the lady of the gun-room—an old man, who kept the gun-room clean. There were the ward-room cooks, and the captain of the sweepers; the captain of the head, and the writer to the first lieutenant; the loblolly-boys, and the sick-bay sentinels. All of these had "all night in," with the reservation that, if all hands were wanted during the night, they should turn out with the rest to the pressing duty on deck.

The topmen, forecastle men, after-guards, and waisters were divided into two watches, larboard and starboard. They slept at night in hammocks on the lower-deck, packed like sardines, row after row, stretching across the ship from side to side. The hammocks during most of Lord Nelson's career were of a dull, brown colour, not unlike the colour of a tanned sail. Afterwards they were made of white canvas, or "twilled sacking," which was kept white by frequent washing. The hammocks were slung by cords to wooden battens or cleats, nailed to the beams above the gun-decks. The rule was "fourteen inches to a man," but some ships afforded sixteen inches, and one or two as much as eighteen. The petty officers, who slept by the ship's side, had each about two feet of space, as "they are not to be pinched." In practice, the rule was not so severe as it sounds. In most ships the watches were berthed alternately, a man of the larboard watch alternating with a man of the starboard watch in each row. of hammocks, so that at night every other hammock in each row was vacant, and the pressure made more tolerable. In those ships in which this rule was not observed the watches slept on their respective sides, jammed together in great discomfort. The berthing of the men on their respective sides of the ship had the further disadvantage of putting the vessel out of trim, by bringing a great weight to one side, instead of spreading it equably.

Each man had two hammocks, one in use and the other clean. Hammocks were shifted and scrubbed once a week, and hung up to dry between the masts. In the morning of each day, at half past seven, the sleepers were roused from their blankets by the boatswain's pipe, the pipes of his mates, and the "All hands. Turn out and save a clue. Out or down here. Rise and shine. Out or down here. Lash and carry." Those who snuggled into their hammocks for an extra minute were promptly cut down, and beaten about the shoulders with colts or cobs. One was expected to turn out at the first sound of the pipe. The sailors generally slept "all standing, like a trooper's horse" —that is, without taking off many of their clothes. The clothes they did take off they generally laid carefully under their pillows, lest the thieves should get them during the night. On turning out, they slung their clothes about them with all speed, and at once set about lashing their hammocks into tight sausage-like rolls. This they performed by a cord, called a hammock lasher. A correctly-lashed hammock was secured by "seven turns," Directly the seven turns were passed the hammock was lowered on deck, the clues, or head and foot supports, were carefully twisted under the lashing, and the sailor slung the roll over his shoulder, and ran on deck to stow it. The hammock nettings, where the hammocks were stowed, ran all round the upper part of the ship, making a sort of bulwark, six or seven feet high, for the protection of the marines and small-arm parties. The quarter-masters, master's mates, and midshipmen superintended the stowing of the hammocks, and rejected every hammock too loosely lashed to pass through a regulation hoop. Each division of the ship stowed their hammocks in certain well-defined parts of the nettings, as the forecastle men on the forecastle, the foretop men under the fore-rigging, and the marines on the poop. Each hammock was numbered on a white painted patch, with a few plain blue letters indicating the station of its owner. During the daytime, in fine weather, the hammocks were left in the nettings, exposed to the sun and wind. In wet or foul weather they were covered with canvas covers, painted white or yellow, and known as hammock cloths. At night, at about 7 or 7.30 p.m., they were piped down—i.e. removed from their places in the nettings, and slung at their respective battens on the berth-deck. The berthings, the places where the men slept, were indicated by custom. The forecastle men slept forward; the foretop men next to the forecastle men; then the main-top men, waisters, and after-guard. The marines either slept aft, just forward of the gun-room, or in the recesses of the orlop, forward of the after cockpit. The idlers stowed themselves away among the men, towards the ship's sides, or in their little nooks below the gun-decks, in the wings and tiers.

For meals, the sailors divided themselves into messes, of from four to eight members apiece. They always messed apart from the marines, for the "guffies," or "jollies," were not very popular among them. Each mess had a narrow mess table, which could be hooked up, out of the way, to the beams above, when not in use. At meal times the mess tables were fixed between the guns, so as to swing with the pitch of the ship. Each sailor had a knife, spoon, and hook-pot, an earthenware bowl, and a platter. The knife he always wore about his person, in a belt or lanyard. The other crockery he kept in a wooden tub, called a mess kid, which was secured to the ship's side. When the ship went into action these tubs were hurried below, out of the way, or flung bodily overboard. The crockery had to be supplied at the sailor's own cost. If "a sudden lurch," during meal times sent the crockery flying he was forced to purchase tin or wooden ware from the purser, to use till he could buy new china. The messes were very friendly and cheery little parties. They liked to be trim and neat, and to make a brave show with their gear. They hated to be seen using the purser's crockery. Each was presided over by that member of the mess who acted as mess cook for the week. The mess cook had to receive the provisions for the mess from the purser, at the daily issuing of victuals. He had to deliver the meat, peas and oatmeal to the cook in good time. On duff-days he mixed the duff in a handkerchief, whistling a tune while he stoned the raisins (if any were issued), so that none should suspect him of eating them. At tea or supper time he drew the grog for the mess, from the sacred tub under the care of the master's mate. What was more, he drew a "cook's portion," or double allowance, for himself, with which he could buy himself all manner of little luxuries. This extra tot of grog made the post of mess cook to be much desired by all hands. It amply compensated them for the trouble and anxieties of the office.

In some ships the berths, messes, or spaces between the guns were separated and shut off by small screens of canvas for the greater privacy. At night they would be let down to form little shut-off apartments for the privileged petty officers who slept there. The members of each mess were expected to keep their berth scrupulously clean, free from grease spots, biscuit crumbs, and any mess of oatmeal or soup. One of the men of each mess cleaned up after a meal, to remove any disorder of the kind. A man who found himself among uncongenial messmates had permission to change his mess on the first Sunday in each month. This regulation was very wise and humane, and was much esteemed by the sailors. It was customary to speak to the first lieutenant before making the change, giving some reason for the proposed alteration. Some men, who could not agree with their comrades through some fault of temperament, went from mess to mess, till they had disgusted all hands. They then messed alone, as best they could, in out-of-the-way nooks. Quarrelsome and loose-tongued persons, and all those suspected of being white mice, were ostracised in this way. The mess was the one pleasant place aboard where a man could talk freely and cheerily. A man who violated the sanctity of such a place, by quarrelling, privy gambling, political talk, or incitement to mutiny, was not fit to remain in the community. His presence was a danger to all concerned. The petty officers generally messed in those parts of the lower-deck where they slung their hammocks. The sailors were free to make chums where they would, and to mess where they pleased. They availed themselves of the liberty to some extent, but it must be remembered that party spirit always ran very high aboard these ships. A forecastle man affected to despise a topman; a topman despised an after-guard man, and called him a "silk stocking gentleman," or a "gentleman's son," while a member of the after-guard looked down upon a waister, and called him a "Jimmy Dux," or farmer. All four grades united in despising the marines, calling them "the pipeclays," the "guffies," the "jollies," "the johnny-toe-the-liners." Sailors pretended to have a strong dislike for the members of the sea regiment. They affected to hate them so heartily that they could hardly be induced to use pipe-clay, or to learn the platoon.

The "berth" was not only the place where the seaman ate his meals; it was in many ships the place where he kept his belongings. In frigates, the seamen and marines were

61

allowed to carry small sea chests to sea, one chest to every two men, each chest to lie in its owners' berth, but the permission was cancelled if the chests were insecurely fastened to the side of the ship. In action, of course, these chests were struck down into the hold, out of the way. In line-of-battle ships he was allowed to keep his bag in the berth. In others he had to keep it in a rack in the wings on the orlop-deck, to which access might be had at certain times. In these ships a sailor generally kept a change of clothes in his hammock, so that if he were drenched during the night-watch he might put on dry things when he came below, without waiting till the racks were opened. Some captains were very careful to see that the bags were dried in the sun after heavy weather. Others were needlessly careful to have them all properly numbered, and painted (or even pipe-clayed) alike. It was necessary to keep a very strict watch upon the bags, for all the ships swarmed with thieves, and a bag left about the decks, or left unguarded, was swiftly emptied. Any article left loose upon the deck, and found by a ship's corporal or boatswain's mate, was taken to the quarter-deck, and exposed to the ship's company. If the owner claimed it he had his grog stopped, or weakened. If the owner did not claim it it was sold at the next sale of dead men's effects.

The sailor's kit was a very simple affair. He had a hammock, with or without a "donkey's breakfast," or straw mattress, covered by two thick blankets. Pillow and hammock stretcher were merely matters of personal taste. Sheets were unknown, save in some of the sick-bays. For foul weather he had a short wrap-rascal coat of "rug" or frieze, and a leathern or thick felt or tarred canvas apron, reaching below the knee. Sea boots, coming to the knee or thigh, were never worn by the seamen. In foul weather they wore their ordinary low shoes, with extra thick woollen stockings and knee-breeches, a rig no more uncomfortable than the sea boot, and fully as effective in keeping the legs dry. In fine weather, when ashore, the sailor usually wore a short, round, very smart blue jacket, with a row of flat gold or bright brass buttons down the right side and on the cuffs. His trousers were either of blue cloth, or of white duck, cut extremely loose, and a shade too long, so that they nearly covered the feet. These garments were kept in position by a sheath-knife belt, or by a black silk handkerchief knotted round the waist. The stockings were frequently of good white silk, for a sailor loved to have fine silk stockings. The shoes were not unlike our modern black dancing pumps, save that big silver buckles took the place of silk bows. The shirt was the least stereotyped article of dress. A shirt or jersey of blue and white horizontal stripes was popular. A white shirt with large red or blue spots had many admirers. Some wore plain red or plain blue, and some may even have worn white. The throat of the shirt had a loose, unstarched collar, which was worn open, in the Byronic manner. Round the throat, very loosely knotted, was a fine black silk handkerchief, the ends of which dangled over the lapels of the waistcoat. The waistcoat was generally of scarlet kerseymere, cut very low and very long. Canary-yellow waistcoats were common, and some wore spotted or striped ones. It depended mostly on the stock committed to the purser for his slop-room. The sailors were very fond of decorating both jacket and waistcoat with coloured ribbons, which they sewed down the seams, to give a more gay effect. For the ordinary work about decks they wore white duck or blue cloth trousers, and blue, green or red serge, duch or flannel frocks. A jacket of a coarse yellow stuff appears in some pictures, in conjunction with striped trousers (blue and white). For hat, the usual wear ashore was a little low tarpaulin hat, kept black and glossy with tar and oil, and cut in a shape dimly resembling the top-hats worn by our bishops and busmen, but with a more knowing rake. This hat had often a broad black ribbon dangling from it, bearing the name of the ship in white letters. When at work aboard the sailor sometimes wore a painted straw hat, with black silk ribbons flung rakishly "over the left eye." More often he wore a fur cap, or a battered, soft, shore beaver, or a low-crowned felt hat, with the brim curled up. Woollen tam-o'-shanters were sometimes worn, but the fur cap was the most popular headgear during working hours. The fur cap had flaps, which could be unbuttoned and let down so as to protect the ears. Some sailors wore a sort of turban, made of a red or yellow handkerchief, twisted about the head. Others wore a sort of woollen nightcap or jacobin cap. The headgear, whatever it was, was nearly always worn well to the back of the head, as though it balanced "on three hairs." The narrow-minded have judged that this fashion sprang from the natural levity and savagery of the mariners. As a matter of fact, a sailor found it difficult to wear his hat in any other way. He was continually looking aloft or running aloft or working aloft, and it would have been impossible for him to wear his headgear in any other position. One cannot run up rigging with a hat jammed down over one's eyes.

It must be remembered that this outfit varied with the individual. Only those who bought from the slop chest wore "uniform." Those who brought decent shore-going clothes aboard were generally free to wear them, though some captains insisted that their men should all wear frocks or shirts of the same colours. The shore-going dress we have indicated was certainly worn by the smartest of our sailors, for Captain Brenton describes some poor fellows coming up for trial, as "tall and athletic, well dressed, in blue jackets, red waistcoats, and trousers white as driven snow," with "their hair like the tail of a lion," hanging "in a cue down their back....the distinguishing mark of a thoroughbred seaman."

The days of which we write were the days of clean-shaving. Officers and men alike shaved their cheeks and upper lips. A hairy man was not to be tolerated. But though the men shaved themselves daily they liked to wear their hair long, either falling down the shoulders in a mass, or braided into a queue, with some grease and black silk ribbon. It is not known when the use of the pigtail became general, it seems to have been borrowed from the French. It may possibly have been borrowed from the marines, who wore pomatum-stiffened pigtails, or pigtails stiff with grease and flour, during this period. From 1800 to 1815 the pigtail seems to have been popular, after that time it gradually fell into disuse. The sailors dressed each other's queues, turn and turn about. It took an hour "to dress and be dressed." It is not known whether the sailors ever used flour to whiten the queues when plaited, but probably they wore them plain. Those who had but little hair made false queues of teased-out oakum, which was sufficiently good imitation to pass muster. Many sailors, who did not care for pig-tails, wore most ravishing curls or love-locks over their ears, like the ladies in a book of beauty. A number of them wore earrings, "of the most pure gold," which they bought from the Jews at Portsmouth. They wore them less for decoration than for a belief they held that their use improved the sight. Some captains forbade the use of earrings on the ground that they were un-English.

The food issued to the sailors was nearly always bad, and sometimes villainous. The following table gives the scale of provisions generally issued:—

	Biscuit lbs. avoir.	Beer gallons	Beef lbs.	Pork lbs.	Pease pints	Oat-meal pints	Sugar oz.	Butter oz.	Cheese oz.
Sunday	1	1	—	1	½	—	—	—	—
Monday	1	1	—	—	—	½	2	2	4
Tuesday	1	1	2	—	—	—	—	—	—
Wednesday	1	1	—	—	½	½	2	2	4
Thursday	1	1	—	1	½	—	—	—	—
Friday	1	1	—	—	½	½	2	2	2
Saturday	1	1	2	—	—	—	—	—	—
	7	7	4	2	2	1½	6	6	12

The provisions were nearly always issued on a reduced scale. It was the general custom to mess the men "six upon four," an arrangement by which six men received and lived upon, the allowance of four men. The sailors were allowed certain moneys for the food withheld from them; this allowance was called "savings money." The food was of bad quality and by no means liberally given. The sailor's chief stand-by was the sea air, which somehow never fails, even aboard modern merchant-men. The biscuit was the most liberal ration, for few sailors ate the whole of the allowance, even on the reduced proportion. That which they could not eat they returned either to the purser, in exchange for savings money, or held as an asset, to exchange for fruit and the like when the ship arrived in a foreign port. The biscuit was cooked in the royal bakeries, attached to the dockyards—70 biscuits, weighing 4 oz. apiece, were made each minute in these works. They were round, thick, well-browned biscuits, stamped with a perforator in the centre, so that the centre was much more compressed, and therefore tougher than the remainder. The centre was generally the last piece eaten. It was known as a "reefer's nut." Often enough it was hove overboard. Most biscuits were made of mixed wheat and pea-flour, with sometimes a base addition of bone-dust. The pea-flour generally worked itself into yellow lumps and veins, of an incredible hardness, which could not be bitten through until the biscuit had become soft through long keeping. When the biscuit did become soft, it took to itself an unpleasant, musty, sourish taste, and began to attract, or to breed, weevils. On a long passage, in a hot climate, the "bread" became unspeakably bad, and as full of maggots as it could hold. Re-baking, in the ship's ovens, sometimes remedied the evil, but the most common custom was to leave the creatures to their quiet, and to eat the biscuit at night, when the eye saw not, and the tender heart was spared. Now and then the mess cooks made savoury dishes out of the ship's biscuit, by soaking it in water, and frying it with little strips, or gobbets, of pork fat. Or they enclosed it in a canvas bag, and pounded it, with crows or marline-spikes, till it was as fine as coarse flour. They then mixed it with chopped-up meat, and bribed the cook to bake it. Sometimes they mixed the pounded biscuit with pork-fat and sugar, and made a delectable cake. The cook would always consent to bake these little delicacies, for some small consideration, such as a little grog from the mess he obliged, or a little piece of the dainty.

The badness of the meat may be guessed from the fact that the sailors spoke of it as junk, or old condemned hemp rope. It may not have been bad when cut up and put in cask, but there was an invariable rule in the navy that "the old meat should be eaten first." A ship's company had to start a cruise upon the old meat returned from various ships and routed out from the obscure cellars of the victualling yards. Frequently it had been several years in salt before it came to the cook, by which time it needed rather a magician than a cook to make it eatable. It was of a stony hardness, fibrous, shrunken, dark, gristly, and glistening with salt crystals. It was "believed to be salt horse, resembling very much a piece of mahogany, and often quite as sapless." It looked as unwholesome as meat could look. Strange tales were told about it. Old pigtailed seamen would tell of horseshoes found in the meat casks; of curious barkings and neighings heard in the slaughter-houses; and of negroes who disappeared near the victualling yards, to be seen no more. Whatever meat it may have been, the salt beef was certainly abominable. It could, perhaps, have been made eatable by long soaking in the steep tub, but no meat for the messes was ever soaked for more than twenty-four hours. The salt pork was generally rather better than the beef, but the sailors could carve fancy articles, such as boxes, out of either meat. The flesh is said to have taken a good polish, like some close-grained wood. The beef was sometimes chopped up fine, and used for the flavouring in "sea pies," or "dry hashes"—two dishes the sailors sometimes made for themselves, and persuaded the cook to dress. The meat ration was not only bad, but extremely small. The 4-lb. pieces with which the casks were filled were not by any means pure meat. They were mostly bone, fat, and gristle. The pound of flesh, as issued to the sailor, was often seven-tenths uneatable. The fat was dirty, and provocative of scurvy. The bone and gristle could only be thrown overboard. At best, a sailor could but hope to find a few salt fibres of meat, hidden away snugly—like good deeds in a naughty world—under layers of evil-looking fat. They were not enough to give the poor mariner a feeling that he had had meat for dinner. But if he wished to have meat for supper, "to make him taste his wine well," he had to save some from his midday meal. Some were even so provident as to remember the starvation breakfast, and to stint themselves at tea and dinner in order to have a feast the next morning. Those who did not care for grog were the lucky ones, for these had always half-a-pint of rum with which to buy the meat of the drinkers. Many were the little bargains made about the mess tables, at the blessed supper time, when the roll of the drum had sent aft the mess cooks to the tub. "Bill, I'll swop my whack of beef to-morrow for half yours." "Joe, I'll give you my pea-soup for your grog." "Tom, I'll mix your duff for you if you'll give me just a nip." etc. etc.

The mess cook, who acted as carver and parter of the food, was at all times most equitable in his duty. While he cut up the meat, or divided the allowance, whatever it was, he ordered one of the mess to turn his back, and shut his eyes. When a whack or portion had been cut or placed on a plate he called out: "Who shall have this?" The blindfolded man then pronounced the name of one of the messmates, and the portion, whether too big or too small, was at once allotted to the man thus named. The system was as fair as any that could be devised.

The pea-soup, which was issued on salt pork days, was "somehow always good." It was generally eaten hot, but some preferred to save it till the evening, when they took it cold, as a relish to the grog and biscuit. The "burgoo," "skillagolee," or oatmeal gruel, issued to the men for breakfast, was invariably bad. The greatest proportion of it went to the pigstys, as uneatable by mortal man. It was issued by the Government at the insistence of some medical adviser, who thought that it would act as a "corrective" to "acid and costive humours." The oatmeal was of a pretty bad quality to begin with, but by the time the cook had wreaked his wicked will upon it, by boiling it in his coppers with the unspeakable ship's water, the mess had become disgusting beyond words. Few of the sailors could eat it in its penetrating, undisguised nastiness, and, according to a naval surgeon, it was "cruel to expect them to do so." In later years, after Trafalgar, a small proportion of molasses, or butter, was issued with the oatmeal, to be eaten with it, to render it less nauseous. Without the butter and molasses it was fitter for the pigstys than for men. Many messes would not draw the ration, but preferred to have the money for it at the end of the cruise. Another favourite breakfast dish was Scotch coffee, or burnt ship's biscuit boiled in water, to a thick blackish paste, and sweetened with sugar. There was also a ration of very villainous cocoa, with which the sailors received a little brown sugar. On one of these dishes the jolly sailor had to make his breakfast. He seldom received anything else at that meal, save the biscuit in the mess's bread barge, unless he had deprived himself of dinner and supper the day before in order to have a bite of meat. At the beginning of each cruise in home waters he received a very small allowance of ship's butter. This was kept in a mess tin, and equally shared. It was of poor quality, as butter, and grew a great deal worse as the days passed. After a month or two at sea it was at its very worst. It was then solemnly routed out and inspected, condemned as putrid, and given to the boatswain for the anointment of shrouds and running rigging. For dinner the men received their salt beef and pork, their pea-soup, and their occasional duffs. On two days a week (if not more frequently) they held a fast, receiving no meat. These days were known as "banyan" days—a "banyan" being a thin kind of duck frock, suitable for the tropics, but uncomfortable elsewhere. For supper they sometimes received a ration of strong ship's cheese, the most abominable stuff imaginable. It would not keep at sea. It smelt very horribly, and, what was worse, it bred long, thin, red worms before it had been a month in the ship's hold.

Though the solids were not very choice the liquids were sometimes really good. The water was bad—so bad that few could drink it without disgust—but one drank no water aboard ship so long as the beer held out. The water was generally river water. We note that the river water "about London" was reckoned especially good. It was carried to sea, not in iron tanks, as it is carried nowadays, but in wooden casks, not over clean. Sometimes the casks were found to be old oil casks. The water invariably became putrid after standing in cask for a few days. It then grew sweet again, and fit to drink, but after standing and working for several weeks in the hold it became thick and slimy, full of "green grassy things," besides being stagnant and flat. At this stage in its development it was generally tapped for the ship's company. At the beginning of a voyage the company drank beer—small beer, of poor quality, not at all the sort of stuff to put the souls of three butchers into one weaver. It was bad beer, but it was perhaps better than the water. At anyrate it gave a new taste to the mouths of the poor seamen, who got very tired of the perpetual salt food and biscuit. The beer generally lasted for a month, during which time no wine or spirits was issued. In port the sailors used to fortify the ship's beer with rum or brandy, making a very potent drench called flip, which was popular among their lady friends, who used to smuggle aboard the necessary spirits. If the sailors wanted a drink at any time during the night-watch they used to go to a small cask called a scuttle butt, in which fresh water was kept. A tin cup was secured to the cask, so that the men might drink in comfort. No one was allowed to draw fresh water from this cask for the purpose of washing his clothes.

When all the beer had been expended, the captains allowed the issue of wines or spirits. A pint of wine, or half-a-pint of rum or brandy, was considered the just equivalent of a gallon of beer. The wine in use was of very ordinary vintage. It was often purchased abroad, and varied with the port of purchase. The sailors seem to have preferred white wine. They disliked the red wines issued to them in the Mediterranean. They called them "Black Strap." To be stationed in the Mediterranean was "to be black-strapped." Their favourite wines were two cheap Spanish wines: "rosolio" and "mistela," the latter a fiery white wine, affectionately known as "Miss Taylor." But when the beer had gone, and the wine had been drunken, there was yet "the sailor's sheet anchor"—grog. At noon each day, when spirits were being served, "the fifer was called to play 'Nancy Dawson,' or some other lively tune," to give notice that the tub was ready. The cook of each mess attended with a flagon, in which to fetch the precious fluid to his mates. The noon allowance was one gill of pure navy rum mixed with three gills of water, a little lemon acid, as an anti-scorbutic, and a dash of sugar. The supper allowance was issued in the same proportions, though without the sugar and lemon juice. Grog time was the pleasantest part of the day. With a gill of good spirits beside, or inside him, a sailor thought foul scorn of the boatswain's mate, and looked upon the world with charity. He was not allowed to drink, or to receive, his beloved liquid in a dram (i.e. neat), but by the exercise of a little patience he was able to obtain a most decided feeling from its imbibition. A gill was not enough to turn an old seaman's head, but by saving up the gill till supper, and adding to it the second gill, with any third gill purchased or acquired from a shipmate, the oldest sailor found it possible to believe himself an admiral. Often enough at this stage he found it difficult to lie on the deck without holding on. It is not wonderful that so many men got drunk aboard the King's ships at this time. For about a month before Christmas day, which was always held as a general holiday and feast of Bacchus, the sailors saved up their grog, half-a-gill a day, till they had enough to paralyse every sentient thing below-decks. The officers kept clear on Christmas day, for "a wet Christmas" was a very lively experience. Nearly every man aboard got into "a state of beastly intoxication." Drunken men lay in heaps under the hatches, where they had fallen. The lower-deck became a picture of hell. It was no unusual thing to find two or three men dead when the decks were cleared the next morning. The allowance of grog was certainly too large. The sailors were ashamed to allow any of the ration to remain undrunken. They preferred to be flogged at the gangway rather than to waste the good liquor. "In hot climates," says Captain Hall, "I really do not think it an exaggeration to say that one-third of every ship's company were more or less intoxicated, or at least muddled and half stupefied, every evening." It seems curiously hard that men so eager to get drunk should have been so urgently encouraged to drink, and so brutally punished for drinking the drink allowed to them.

The sailors who did not care for grog were generally able to purchase tea or cocoa from those who were less squeamish. Tea and cocoa were not regular rations, but most ships carried them, to issue to the sailors in lieu of the bad cheese sometimes given for supper. A tea drinker could count on getting a quarter of a pound of tea a week when the cheese had become uneatable. All sailors received a weekly half-pint of vinegar, and the temperance man used to buy up the allowance of the mess, and brew a cool drink for himself by mixing the vinegar with water. This brew, tea, and cocoa, were the usual temperance drinks. Few men cared to drink the ship's water undisguised.

It must be remembered that the scale of provisions was often modified by substitutes. Once a week, at least, the beef ration was reduced to one pound, and an equal weight of flour issued with it, to enable the men to make a duff, doughboy, or pudding. Sometimes raisins and currants were given with the flour, but more often the flour was merely mixed with fat, and boiled till it looked like pipeclay, when it was considered

THE SAILOR'S PRAYER!!

O, MIGHTY NEPTUNE! hear an honeſt Britiſh Tar—thou knoweſt I trouble not thy Godſhip every day, I therefore pray thee to grant my Prayer, for I love not long palavering and that there, d'ye ſee.

Grant me a ſtout ſhip, and honeſt Meſſmates—as the laſt of my old ones was popped off the Belerophon's bows at the Nile—poor Mat Mizen!! Give me plenty of Grog, and a good Commander, and I'll warrant you I'll ſhave the Don's whiſkers, and as to MOUNSEER, if I comes athwart his hauſer again, I'll ſhiver his Jib, and dowſe his three-coloured rag, and revenge the death of Mat Mizen, d——n me—I beg your honour's pardon for ſwearing, but its a way I have—however, I ſtill ſay, if I get into *Mounſeer's* wake, I'll back his top-ſails, ſplit my Timbers.

Worthy Maſter Neptune! ſend us a good prize, I beſeech thee, and be not ſparing in Brandy and Tobacco—give us alſo a few cheſts of the Don's Dollars, for Mounſeer ha'nt got none, no more than there is in your honour's three-pronged boat-hook. When we arrive at Port, ſend us handſome Doxies, and keep us from a lee-ſhore, that thou knoweſt I hate as I do an empty can, or a dry quid. Grant me but theſe, and capſize my Trunions if I don't ever praiſe thee, and the Meſſmate that wont join me, may he be ſtuck upon the lee-yard arm of a ſtormy night! Laſtly, I pray thee to keep me from the diſgrace of the Bilboes—ſave me from a Guinea-man and a Tender, and I'll ſerve cheerfully, and ſing King George and his Navy for ever.—Huzza! to the end of the Chapter.

SPRAGG, PRINTER, 27, BOW-STREET, COVENT-GARDEN.

Plate 7 *The Sailor's Prayer*

Plate 8 *The Trafalgar Garter — England expects every man to do his duty.*

cooked. Beans were sometimes given instead of pease. Rice was often given instead of oatmeal, cheese, pease, or ship's biscuit. Sugar was sometimes given instead of butter; barley instead of oatmeal, and oil instead of cheese. In port, fresh beef, mutton, and vegetables were always given to the company, if such articles were readily obtainable. A captain generally tried to vary the provisions issued, as far as he could, for the monotony of alternating pork and beef, both salt and dry, is very unpleasant. The sailors get to crave for a fresh taste, a violent taste, strong enough to clear the mouth of the unpleasant taste with which one wakes in ones hammock. A landsman can hardly imagine the pleasure of sucking a lump of sugar after a month on salt victuals. It was, perhaps, as much the sameness of the ship's provisions as the emptiness of the life which sent the sailors to the grog jack for solace. In port they turned at once to the most strongly-flavoured articles their money could buy. They bought red herrings and onions, good honest stuff, which one could really taste. They drank any villainous compound they could find, from Riga balsam and eau de Cologne to mixed vitriol and cider. Perhaps it was to obtain a fresh taste that they chewed so much strong plug tobacco. They would sometimes chew oakum when the supply of tobacco failed. Some of the sailors had a craving for slush, the melted salt fat from the beef and pork. When a ship's copper was tallowed, or when the topmen were greasing down the rigging, the men had to be watched, and prevented from swallowing the stuff, which was very deleterious, and highly productive of scurvy.

The mess cooks, who did the cooking and carving, also did the washing-up. On Sundays, they cleaned the mess tables, and laid 'out the crockery for inspection. If a mess cook spoiled the duff, or failed to keep the gear clean, he was tried by a jury of mess cooks, gathered "by hoisting a mess swab, or beating a tin dish between-decks forward." The punishments these juries inflicted were of the usual brutal kind.

In addition to the complements of sailors, all ships of war carried a proportion of marines, under their proper officers. The sea regiment was founded at the end of the seventeenth century, not as a permanent force, but as a force in which the King's seamen could be trained. In the first years of the marines they were really young sailors, who went aloft, did the musketry exercise, and joined in the working of the ship. Gradually they lost their sailor craft, and became more and more a military body. They came to be employed less as sailors than as ship's police, a sort of armed guard, ready to repress any mutiny among the tarry-breeks. They were then messed and berthed apart from the sailors, who began to despise them, as an inferior and useless race. In the war years of the late eighteenth and early nineteenth centuries the marines were employed as checks upon the seamen. All ships of war carried them, the proportion varying from about 170 officers and men, in a first-rate, to 140 or 130, in a third-rate, and a dozen, in command of a sergeant in a 10-gun brig. The proportion of marines was therefore about one to every four sailors and idlers. They were usually on friendly terms with the sailors, in spite of the sailors' contempt for pipeclay. Many marines were so eager to learn the sailors' duty that they were allowed to go aloft. In some ships they were allowed to furl the main-sail. When at sea they helped the after-guard in various light duties. They stood sentry-go outside the captain's cabin, magazine hatchways, and in various other parts of the ship, such as the galley door while dinner was cooking. In action they fell in with their muskets on the poop, quarter-deck, and gangways, to gall the enemy's sail-trimmers and topmen, and to give a hand at the braces, if occasion arose. A marine private was dressed in the scarlet tunic of a soldier, with white tight breeches and black Hessian boots. His hat was a sort of top-hat, made of black felt, with gold lace round the brim, a narrow gold band round the crown, and a smart cockade on the left side. A black japanned cartridge box was slung behind him, on two pipeclayed, crossed shoulder-straps. The marine officer wore a smart scarlet tail-coat, with elaborate cuffs and lapels, tight white breeches, low shoes, and silk stockings. In peace time, when not attached to a ship, the marines were not disbanded, but sent to barracks. They were a standing force. When a ship was commissioned they were usually the first part of the crew to come aboard. It was generally their fortune to do all the dirty work connected with the fitting out of the ship. They were at all times subject to the same discipline as the sailors. If they transgressed the rules of the service they were flogged at the gangway like the sailors. They stood no watch at sea, save the occasional sentry-go at the magazines and cabins. They were always berthed far aft on the berth-deck,[1] where they would not be disturbed by the changing watches. Their officers messed in the ward-room, and had little cabins on the lower or orlop deck.

1 *Or on the orlop.*

Chapter VI

Sea Punishments / The cat / Flogging at the gangway /
Flogging through the fleet / Running the gauntlet /
Keel-hauling / Hanging

The punishment most in use in the fleet was flogging on the bare back with the cat-o'-nine-tails. The cat was a short, wooden stick, covered with red baize. The tails were of tough knotted cord, about two feet long. The thieves' cat, with which thieves were flogged, had longer and heavier tails, knotted throughout their length. Flogging was inflicted at the discretion of the captain. It was considered the only punishment likely to be effective with such men as manned the royal ships. It is now pretty certain that it was as useless as it was degrading. Lord Charles Beresford has said that, "in those days we had the cat and no discipline; now we have discipline and no cat." Another skilled observer has said that "it made a bad man worse, and broke a good man's heart." It was perhaps the most cruel and ineffectual punishment ever inflicted. The system was radically bad, for many captains inflicted flogging for all manner of offences, without distinction. The thief was flogged, the drunkard was flogged, the laggard was flogged. The poor, wretched topman who got a ropeyarn into a buntline block was flogged. The very slightest transgression was visited with flogging. Those seamen who had any pride remaining in them went in daily fear of being flogged. Those who had been flogged were generally callous, careless whether they were flogged again, and indifferent to all that might happen to them. It was a terrible weapon in the hands of the officer. In many cases the officers abused the power, by the infliction of excessive punishment for trifling offences. The sailors liked a smart captain. They liked to be brought up to the mark, and if a captain showed himself a brave man, a good seaman, and a glutton for hard knocks, they would stand any punishment he chose to inflict, knowing that such a one would not be unjust. They hated a slack captain, for a slack captain left them at the mercy of the underlings, and that, they said, was "hell afloat." But worse than anything they hated a tyrant, a man who flogged his whole ship's company for little or no reason, or for the infringement of his own arbitrary rules. Such a man, who kept his crew in an agony of fear, hardly knowing whether to kill themselves or their tyrant, was dreaded by all. He was not uncommon in the service until the conclusion of the Great War. It was his kind who drove so many of our men into the American navy. It was his kind who did so much to cause the mutinies at the Nore and Spithead, the loss of the *Hermione* frigate, and (to some extent) the losses we sustained in the American War. Lastly, it was his kind who caused so many men to desert, in defiance of the stern laws against desertion. That kind of captain was the terror of the fleet. We do not know what percentage of captains gave the lash unmercifully. Jack Nastyface tells us that of the nine ships of the line he sailed aboard only two had humane commanders. These two received services of plate from the sailors under their command at the paying-off of their ships; the other seven, we are to presume, ranged from the severe to the brutal.

After all, the cat was not essential to discipline. This was proved time and time again while it was most in use. There were, of course, stubborn, brutal, and mutinous sailors. A fleet so manned could not lack such men. When such men were brought before Lord Nelson, he would say: "Send them to Collingwood. He will tame them, if no one else can." Lord Collingwood was the man who swore, by the god of war, that his men should salute a reefer's coat, even when it were merely hung to dry. Yet he didn't tame his men by cutting their backs into strips. He would have his whole ship's company in perfect order, working like machines, with absolute, unquestioning fidelity. But he seldom flogged more than one man a month, and punished really serious offences, such as drunkenness, inciting to mutiny, and theft, with six, nine, or at most a dozen, lashes. His system tamed the hardest cases in the fleet—good men, whom Lord St Vincent would have flogged to death, or sent to the yard-arm. In conclusion we may quote one of those who saw the last days of flogging: "My firm conviction is that the bad man was very little the better; the good man very much the worse. The good man felt the disgrace, and was branded for life. His self-esteem was permanently maimed, and he rarely held up his head or did his best again." Such was the effect of the favourite punishment in the time of the consulship of Plancus.

Those who transgressed the rules of the ship or of the service during the day were put upon the report of the master-at-arms. The names were submitted by that officer to the first lieutenant, who passed them to the captain every forenoon. Drunkards and mutinous subjects generally passed a night in irons under the half-deck, in the care of an armed marine, before coming up for sentence. Every forenoon, at about half-past ten, those who were on the report went below for their smartest clothes, in the hope that a neat appearance might mollify the captain. Those who were in irons got their messmates to bring them their clothes. At six bells, or eleven o'clock in the forenoon, the captain came on deck, with a paper bearing the names of all delinquents. He bade the lieutenant turn the hands aft to witness punishment. The lieutenant sent a midshipman to the boatswain's mates, and the order was piped and shouted. The marines fell in upon the poop, with their muskets and side-arms. The junior officers gathered to windward under the break of the poop. The captain and lieutenants stood on the weather quarter-deck. The ship's company fell in anyhow, on the booms, boats, and lee-side of the ship directly forward of the main-mast. The doctor and purser fell in to leeward, under the break of the poop, with the boatswain and boatswain's mates in a little gang in front of them. The captain's first order was "rig the gratings." The carpenter and carpenter's mates at once dragged aft two of the wooden gratings which covered the hatches. One of these was placed flat upon the deck. The other was placed upright, and secured in that position against the ship's side or poop railings. When the gratings had been reported rigged the captain called forward the first offender on his list, and told him that he had transgressed the rules of the service, knowing the penalty. He asked the man if he had anything to say in extenuation. If he had nothing to say the order was "Strip." The man flung off his shirt, and advanced bare-shouldered to the gratings, and extended his arms upon the upright. The captain then gave the order "Seize him up." The quarter-masters advanced, with lengths of spun-yarn, with which they tied the man's hands to the grating. They then reported "Seized up, sir." At this point the captain produced a copy of the Articles of War, and read that Article which the offender had infringed. As he read he took off his hat, to show his respect for the King's commandments. Every man present did the same. While the Article was being read one of the boatswain's mates undid a red baize bag, and produced the red-handled cat, with which he was to execute punishment. At the order "Do your duty," he advanced to the man at the grating, drew the cat tails through his fingers, flung his arm back, and commenced to flog, with his full strength, at the full sweep of his arm. He was generally a powerful seaman, and he knew very well that any sign of favouritism would infallibly cause his disrating, if it did not subject him to the same torture. Some seamen could take a dozen, or, as they expressed it, "get a red checked shirt at the gangway," without crying aloud. But the force of each blow was such that the recipient had the breath knocked clean out of him "with an involuntary Ugh." One blow was sufficient to take off the skin, and to draw blood wherever the knots fell. Six blows were enough to make the back positively raw. Twelve blows cut deeply into it, and left it a horrible red slough, sickening to look upon. Yet three dozen was a common punishment. Six dozen lashes were counted as nothing. Three hundred lashes were very frequently given.

Before a severe punishment the sufferer's messmates used to bring him their tots of grog, saved up from supper the night before, so that he might at least begin his torture in blessed stupefaction. After a severe punishment they took the poor mangled body down to the sick-bay, and left it there in the care of the surgeon. A body that had been severely lashed looked something like raw veal. It generally healed up, but for weeks after the punishment the sufferer's life was a misery to him, for reasons which may be read in the proper place, but which need not be quoted here.

It may interest some people to know what the punishment felt like. A ruffian has left it on record that it was "nothing but an O, and a few O my Gods, and then you can put on your shirt." It was more than that. A very hardy fellow may have found a dozen or so comparatively easy to bear. But when the lashes ran into the scores it became a different matter. We will quote a poor soldier who was flogged in 1832 with a cat precisely similar to that used in the King's fleet.

"I felt an astounding sensation between the shoulders under my neck, which went to my toe-nails in one direction, and my finger-nails in another, and stung me to the heart, as if a knife had gone through my body....He came on a second time a few inches lower, and then I thought the former stroke was sweet and agreeable compared with that one....I felt my flesh quiver in every nerve, from the scalp of my head to my toenails. The time between each stroke seemed so long as to be agonising, and yet the next came too soon....The pain in my lungs was more severe, I thought, than on my back. I felt as if I would burst in the internal parts of my body....I put my tongue between my teeth, held it there, and bit it almost in two pieces. What with the blood from my tongue, and my lips, which I had also bitten, and the blood from my lungs, or some other internal part, ruptured by the writhing agony, I was almost choked, and became black in the face....Only fifty had been inflicted, and the time since they began was like a long period of life; I felt as if I had lived all the time of my real life in pain and torture, and that the time when existence had pleasure in it was a dream, long, long gone by.''

Another man, who saw a good deal of flogging in his time, has told us that, after the infliction of two dozen lashes, "the lacerated back looks inhuman: it resembles roasted meat burnt nearly black before a scorching fire." The later blows were not laid on less heartily than the first. The striker cleaned the tails of the cat after each blow, so that they should not clog together with flesh and blood, and thus deaden the effect. A fresh boatswain's mate was put on to flog after each two dozen. Some captains boasted of having left-handed boatswain's mates, who could "cross the cuts" made by the right-handed men.

For striking "an admiral, a commodore, captain, or lieutenant," or "for attempting to escape," no matter what provocation may have been given, the most lenient punishment inflicted was flogging through the fleet. The man was put into the ship's long-boat, and lashed by his wrists to a capstan bar. Stockings were inserted between the wrists and the lashing "to prevent him from tearing the flesh off in his agonies." The other boats of the ship were lowered, and each ship in the harbour sent a boat manned with marines to attend the punishment. The master-at-arms and the ship's surgeon accompanied the victim. Before the boat cast off from the ship the captain read the sentence from the gangway. A boatswain's mate then came down the ladder, and inflicted a certain number of lashes on the man. The boat then rowed away from the ship, to the sound of the half-minute bell, the oars keeping time to the drummer, who beat the rogue's march beside the victim. The attendant boats followed, in a doleful procession, rowing slowly to the same music. On coming to the next ship the ceremony was repeated, after which the poor man was cast off and covered with a blanket, and allowed to compose himself. He received a portion of his torture near each ship in the port, "until the sentence was completed." If he fainted he was plied with wine or rum, or in some cases, taken back to the sick-bay of his ship to recover. In the latter case, he stayed till his back had healed, when he was again led out to receive the rest of the sentence. "After he has been alongside of several ships," says Jack Nastyface, who often saw these punishments, "his back resembles so much putrified liver." Those who lived through the whole of the punishment were washed with brine, cured, and sent back to their duty. But the punishment was so terrible that very few lived through it all. Joshua Davis tells us of a corpse being brought alongside, with the head hanging down and the bones laid bare from the neck to the waist. There were still fifty lashes due to the man, so they were given to the corpse, at the captain's order. Those who died during the infliction of the punishment were rowed ashore, and buried in the mud below the tidemark, without religious rites. Those who survived such fearful ordeals were broken men when they came out of the sick-bay. They lived but a little while afterwards, in a nervous and pitiful condition, suffering acutely in many ways. It is said that those who were flogged through the fleet were offered the alternative of the gallows.

A man caught thieving was generally set to run the gauntlet. The members of the ship's crew formed into a double line right round the main or spar deck. Each man armed himself with three tarry rope yarns, which he twisted up into what was called a knittle or nettle, knotted at the end, and about three feet long. The thief was stripped to the waist, and brought to one end of the line. The master-at-arms stood in front of him, with a drawn sword pointing to his breast. Two ship's corporals stood close behind him, with drawn swords pointing to his back. If he went too quickly or too slowly the sword points pricked him. When he was placed in position at the end of a line a boatswain's mate gave him a dozen lashes with the thieves' cat. He was then slowly walked (or dragged on a grating) through the double line of men, who flogged him with their nettles as he walked past them. When he arrived at the end of a line a boatswain's mate gave him another taste of the thieves' cat, and either started him down another line or turned him back by the way he had come. It was very cruel punishment, for it flayed the whole of the upper part of a man's body, not omitting his head. After running the gauntlet the man went into hospital, to be rubbed with brine and healed. He was then sent back to his duty, "without a stain upon his character." He had purged his offence. It was never again mentioned by his shipmates.

Those who contradicted an officer—or appeared to contradict him, by answering back, however respectfully—were punished by gagging. The lieutenants had no power to flog, but they had power to inflict minor punishments. Gagging was one of those they inflicted on their own initiative. The offender was brought to the rigging, or to the bitts, with his hands tied behind him. An iron marline spike was placed across his mouth, between his teeth, like a bit. The ends were fitted with spun-yarn, which was passed round the head, and knotted there to keep the iron in position. With this heavy piece of iron in his mouth the man had to stand till his mouth was bloody, or till the officer relented. If a man displeased an officer at any time, he was often punished on the spot, by a boatswain's mate. The officer would call a boatswain's mate and say: "Start that man." The boatswain's mate at once produced a hard knotted cord, called a starter, with which he beat the man unmercifully about the head and shoulders, till the officer bade him to desist. The sailors found the starting even harder to bear than the cat, for it generally fell upon their arms as they raised them to protect their heads. It was very severe punishment, and frequently caused such swollen and bruised arms that the sailors could not bear to wear their jackets. It was inflicted with very little cause. Whenever an order was given the boatswain's mates drew out their colts or starters and thrashed the men to their duty with indiscriminating cruelty. It was not lawful punishment, being wholly unauthorised by regulation. But there was no appeal; the sailors had to grin and bear it. After 1811 it was very strictly suppressed.

The boatswain, master-at-arms, and ship's corporals, with their rattans, or supple-jacks, were every whit as ready to thrash the seamen as the boatswain's mates. They, too, carried colts, or starters, made of 3-inch rope, so unlaid that the strands made three knotted tails. With these they beat the seamen for any slight, or fancied slight, until their arms were tired. The sergeant of marines was similarly provided, but his attentions were confined to his own department. He had no power over the bluejackets, except in fifth and sixth rates. Besides all these petty tyrants there were the lesser bullies, the midshipmen, who took delight in torturing the seamen in many ways.

The old-fashioned punishments of ducking from the yard-arm, and keel-hauling, were not practised in our fleet. They had fallen out of use during the eighteenth century, though the French still practised them. Captain Glascock saw a Frenchman keel-hauled early in the last century. Instead of them, there were other punishments, such as a disciplinarian could invent on the spot. Spitting on the decks was discouraged by fastening buckets round the offender's neck, and causing the man to walk the lower deck, as a sort of peripatetic cuspidor. Minor offences were punished by stoppage of grog, or of some part of it; by the infliction of dirty or harassing duty; or by riding a man on a gun with his feet tied together beneath the piece.

Capital offences were expiated at the yard-arm. The man was taken to the cathead, a yellow flag was flown at the masthead, a gun was fired, and all the bad characters of the ship manned the yard-rope, and ran the victim up to the end of the yard.

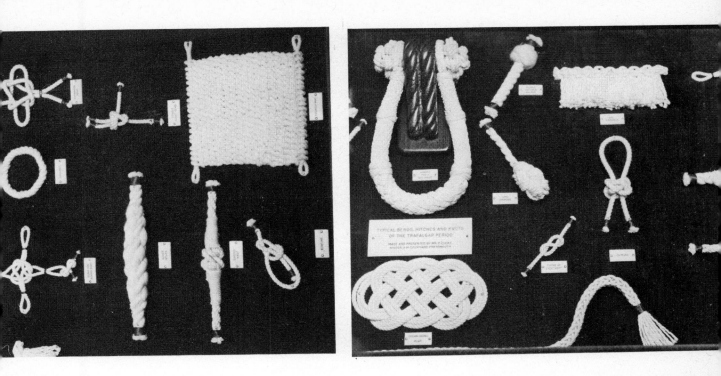

Plate 9 *Knots of the period.*

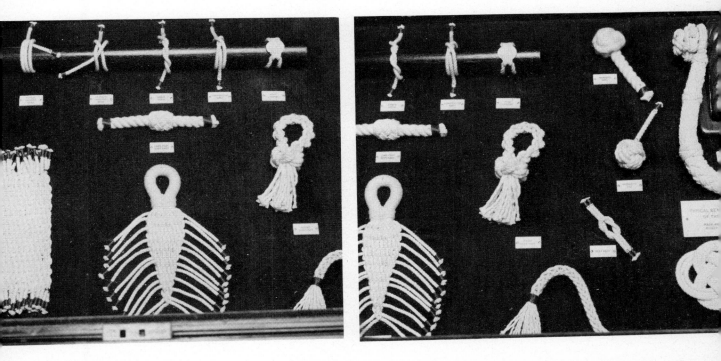

An accurate View (*drawn & etched by J.T. Smith, Engraver of the ANTIQUITIES of* London & Westminster) *from the House of* W. Tunnard, Esq. *on the Bank*
Greenwich **to** Whitehall; *comprehending not only the Vessels attending & the various other objects in*
First Barge, covered with black cloth. The Standard, borne by Capt. Sir Fra. Laforey B.ᵗ Supported by Lieut.ˢ Barker and Antram:
The Guidon, borne by Capt. Baynton (in the absence of Capt. Durham) supported by 2 Lieut.ˢ Rouge croix and Bluemantle
pursuivants. —— Second Barge, cover'd with black Cloth: Heralds of Arms, bearing the Surcoat, Target & Sword, Helm and
Crest & the Gauntlet & Spurs of the deceased: The Banner of the deceased, as K.B. borne by Capt. Rotheram, supp. by 2 Lieut.ˢ
The great Banner, with the augmentations, borne by Capt. Moorsom, supported by Lieut.ˢ Keys & Tucker. —— Third Barge, cov.
with black Velvet, black plumes, &c. Capt. Yule, Atkinson (Master of the Victory) Capt. Williams, Lieut.ˢ Brown & Purches.——
The BODY: Norroy, K. of Arms (in the absence of Clarenceux, indisposed) Union Flag: Attendants on the Body, while

Dear is the Triumph, w
"*Though* Victory *crown*
"*He was ever the defende*
"*mind; and continued his lo*

London, Feb.ʳ 15ᵗʰ 1806, published accordin

Plate 10 *The scene at Nelson's funeral as the funeral barge passed from Greenwich Hospital to St. Paul's Cathedral. Sir Winston Churchill had this scene in mind when he laid down instructions for his own funeral.*

...ing the Scite of Shakspeare's Theatre — on Wednesday the 8th. January, 1806; when the remains of the great ADMIRAL LORD NELSON were brought from
...at Procession; but also the principal Buildings, &c between the Monument & Saint Pauls, inclusive.

...breath must tell —
...t the Hero fell!"

Citizens, both in body &
...ds his countrymen, all his life".
            Maccabees.

...rliament, by J.T.Smith, No. 36, Newman Street.

at Greenwich: Fourth Barge, cov. with blk. Cloth: Chief Mourner Sir Peter Parker, Bt. Adm. of the Fleet, supp. by Adm. Viscount Hood
Adm. Lord Radstock: 6 assistant Mourners, viz. Adm. Caldwell, Curtis, Bligh, Pole, Nugent & Hamilton. 4 Supp. of the Pall, viz.
Vice Adm. Whitshed & Taylor, Adm. Orde (in the absence of Vice Adm. Savage) & Rear Adm. Eliab Harvey: 6 Supp. of the Canopy, viz.
Rear Adm. Drury, Douglas, Wells, Coffin, Aylmer & Domett. Train Bearer to the Chief Mourner, Hon. Henry Blackwood; Windsor Herold
acting for Norroy K of Arms: The Banner of Emblems borne by Capt. Hardy, supported by Lieut. King & Bligh: His Majesty's Barge: The Lords
Commissioners of the Admiralty, their Barge, & immediately after, the City State Barge (the Rt. Hon. James Shaw, Lord Mayor) follow'd
by the Barges of several of the Companies of the City of London.   The Engraver is signally obliged to Francis Townsend Esq Windsor Herold.
                                                    F.A.S. for his liberal communications.

Plate 11 *(a) Nelson recreating with his brave tars after the glorious battle of the Nile, by Rowlandson. Discipline was relaxed for a period immediately after a battle. (b) Nelson, aged fourteen. Artist unknown. (c) Brave Nelson's last lash or a Memento for the Dons, published in December, 1805.*

Chapter VII

In Action

At the first sight of a suspicious ship, all hands were called, and the drummer of the marines beat to quarters. The roll to quarters was short, quick, and determined, being the tune of the song "Hearts of Oak." Directly the drumming ceased the sailors sprang to their tasks. They knew their posts, and the work allotted to them. The ship was cleared quickly and quietly, each man of the hundreds aboard going at once to his place to fit it for battle. The carpenter with his mates, and a number of allotted assistants, repaired aft to the officers' cabins, to unship the wooden bulkheads. The light wooden screens were easily knocked from their grooves, and hurried down into the hold. The captain's furniture, generally no more than a table, settee, and a few chairs, was handed down to the same place, and secured by a rope or two. If the ship had to be cleared in a hurry these things were tossed overboard. The French seem to have left them standing, trusting to fortune to keep the splinters from doing any hurt. Men from each mess went to the lower-deck, to the berth, to clear away the crockery, kit-bags, sea chests, etc., and to run them down out of the way into the wings. The topmen securely "stopped" the top-sail sheets, rove preventer-lifts, slung their lower-yards with chain, prepared their muskets, swivel-guns, pistols and hand-grenades, and got up a few coils of rope and some spare blocks ready for emergencies. If it were dark, or likely to be dark before the fight had been brought to a conclusion, the purser issued "purser's glims." in heavy battle lanterns, one of which was secured to the ship's side by each gun. As the lanterns were liable to be shaken from their places by the concussion of the firing they were secured very tightly. They gave little light; but by the help of the moon, if any shone, and by instinct, and the knowledge of what was to be done, the sailors managed very well. Few actions were fought in the dark, as the risk was too great. It was always well to have a good look at the enemy before engaging.

The hammocks, which ran all round the upper or spar deck, made a good protection to the men engaged upon the gangways. Before going into action, a number of hammocks were taken from the nettings and lashed to the lower rigging, over the dead-eyes and lanyards. A few hammocks were sometimes whipped into the tops, to protect the topmast-rigging in the same way. Strong rope nettings were hung over the upper-deck under the masts, to catch any wreck or men falling from above. Some buckets of water were sent aloft and poured over the sails. Sometimes the engine was rigged, and placed upon the poop, so that the hose played upon

77

the courses. The booms and boats were liberally drenched. The buckets hanging on the quarter-deck were filled, and fire hoses were laid along each deck. Buckets of water were laid by all the hatchways, ready for use. A bucket of fresh water, a tub of salt water, and a swab, were placed behind each gun, for the refreshment of the men, and in case of fire. Wet sand was sprinkled over every deck, to make the planking moist, so as to lessen the risk of fire, and to give surety to the footing of the men. The match tubs were half filled with water. Wet canvas cloths were rolled along the orlop to the mouths of the magazines. Wet frieze screens were then nailed round the magazine hatches, so that no spark could possibly penetrate to them. Wetted blankets were hung round each hatchway.

While the appointed men were doing these things, the captains of the guns went to the gunner's store-rooms to get their cartouche boxes, or square leather cases, filled with the powder tubes or quills, for insertion in the touch-holes of the guns. They also received the flinted gun-locks with which to fire the guns. The men told off to the cannon cast their guns loose from their lashings, struck their ports open, cleared away the side-tackles, preventer-tackles, and breechings, took out the tompions, cast off the leaden aprons, made ready the crows and handspikes, and laid the sponge ready for use. They got the cheeses of wads ready, and placed "garlands," or rope-rings containing round shot, between the guns. Those of the gun's crews who were told off as boarders put a couple of loaded pistols, and a ship's cutlass in their belts. The gun-captains hung up their powder horns, full of priming powder, above their pieces, and stuck their priming-irons into their belts ready for use. The powder-boys brought up their "salt-boxes" full of cartridges for the first broadsides. The marines, or at anyrate some of their number, fell in upon the poop quarter-deck and fore-castle, with their muskets and side-arms. They were expected to shoot the enemy's topmen, and to pick off the musketeers and sail-trimmers on the poop and quarter-deck of the opposing ship. Some of their number helped to work the heavy carronades of the upper after-batteries. The drummers and fifers of the company, who were generally little fellows, younger than the ship's boys, were employed to keep them supplied with powder and ball-cartridge.

Any animals below decks were generally hoisted up and slung overboard, so that the pens in which they lived might be demolished. Hen-coops generally went over the side in the same way. If they were stowed in the boats on the booms, they were allowed to remain. We read of a cock which was liberated by a round shot in time to cheer the ship's company by crowing from the stump of a mast. If there were pigs in the manger, which was a very powerful barricade, little likely to be destroyed, they were suffered to stay there.

It took but a few minutes to clear a ship for action. The guns were cast loose, the lumber cleared away, yards slung, sheets stopped, and the galley-fire extinguished in much less time than a landsman would think possible. As soon as the men had taken their places the lieutenants walked around the gun-decks, to see that all was ready, at the same time giving orders that the guns should be loaded and run out. All this work was done silently: there was no singing out or loud talking. Down below the gun-decks the gunner was busy in his magazines, handing out cartridges to the powder-boys, who put them in the wooden or leathern cases, and carried them to the guns. His mates were kept employed filling fresh cartridges to replace those discharged. The surgeon, with his assistants, prepared the cockpit for the wounded, making ready a number of tourniquets and pledgets for first intentions. A number of tourniquets were distributed about the gun-decks for use by the men who carried down the wounded. As a final preparation, the ship's hatches were tripped up, so that the men could not run below to the security of the orlop-deck. The small fore and after hatches were left standing, to allow the powder-boys and messengers to pass down. They were, however, guarded by marines, who had orders to allow no one save powder-boys and midshipmen to go down by them. Those hatches which led from the gun-deck to the orlop were guarded by midshipmen with pistols, who had orders to shoot any man trying to escape his duty. To prevent anyone from trying to impose upon these hatch-way sentries, it was the rule that all powder-boys going for powder should display their cartridge cases as they reached the ladder. The gunner, also had orders to refuse to give powder to anyone without a proper case.

When all was ready, the lieutenant, and sometimes the captain, made the tour of the decks to cheer the men, and to give their final orders. At the same time the carpenter and his mates took up their stations on the orlop-deck and in the hold, with their shot plugs ready for immediate insertion.

Many of the sailors delighted in battle, not because they were fond of fighting, but because discipline was relaxed during the fight, and, in spite of the extra duty, for a day or two afterwards; and because a victory meant prize-money and a jolly time in port. A fight broke the monotony of a cruise. It made the officers rather more humane in their treatment. Lastly, it was exciting in itself. It was, however, less popular among the men than among the officers. If an officer was badly hurt he got promotion and half pay. If a man was maimed he had nothing but Greenwich Hospital to look for. If he could not get into the hospital he was free to starve, saying with Goldsmith's sailor, that those who got both legs shot off, and a consequent pension, were born with golden spoons in their mouths. Nevertheless, they always went into action cheerily. Their motto was "The hotter the war the sooner the peace," and they knew that they would not be discharged till peace had been declared. Even those who were stationed in the waist or midship guns were merry as they went to quarters. "The very idea of going into action" was "a source of joy to them." They were as brave as they were careless. A hot engagement was meat and drink to them. The thought of a general action kept them from their beds.

It was their custom, when going into action, to strip to the waist. They took their black silk handkerchiefs, and bound them very tightly round their heads over their ears, so that the roar of the guns might not deafen them for life. It was remarked that men going into action always wore a sullen frown, however merry they were in their talk. Before the firing began they used to settle among themselves what amount of prize-money they would win, and how they would spend it. They also made their wills, not in writing, but verbally:

If they get me, Jack, you can have my kit. Tom, you can have my trousers to buy you a mourning ring," etc., always merrily, as though the prospect of death was very remote. They would also whisper to each other, as they came down to the enemy, as to her strength, size, and appearance, guessing her nationality, length of absence from home, etc., from the cut and shape of her masts and sails, and the colour of the bunt patches in her top-sails.

It is not known how a gun-deck looked during the heat of an engagement; for those who saw most of the fighting have left us but a poor account of their experiences. We may take Smollett's word for it, that it was "a most infernal scene of slaughter, fire, smoke and uproar." We can imagine fifteen or sixteen cannon in a row, all thundering and recoiling and flashing fire; on the other side of the ship a similar row, nearly certain to be thundering and flashing fire, if the action were general, instead of a duel between ships. Up above, immediately overhead, not more than a foot from one's hat crown, was a similar double row of cannon, with heavy carriages which banged and leaped at each recoil. Up above those, perhaps, if the ship were a first or second rate, was yet another gun-deck, with its thundering great guns and banging gun-trucks. And above that, as a sort of pendant, was the upper battery of carronades, making a terrible roaring at each shot; and marines firing their muskets, and topmen firing their swivels, and blocks and spars and heavy ropes coming down from aloft with a clatter. And every now and again, if not every minute, the awful ear-splitting crash, "like the smashing of a door with crowbars," as a shot struck home, and sent the splinters scattering. Then, continually, the peculiar hissing and screaming of the passing round shot made a lighter music, "like the tearing of sails," to the bass of the cannon. One heard, too, the yells of perhaps five or six hundred men, as they tugged at the tackling, or hove the guns round with the handspikes. Then there were wounded men screaming, and port-lids coming down with a bang, and perhaps a gun bursting, or thudding clean out of its carriage, as a shot struck a trunnion; and every now and then a horrible noise, as a ball exploded a cartridge on the deck.

So much for the racket. The noise was the clearest impression one could gather. One could see little enough when once the firing had begun. A large ship, fighting only one broadside at a time, burned from 500 to 1100 lbs. of powder every minute, according to the heat of the battle and the distance of the target. It was black powder, and the decks were black with smoke after the first broadside, if they were engaging to windward, for the smoke blew back at the ports, and poured up the hatches like the reek of factory chimneys. In the murk and stench one might see the flash from the spouting touch-holes, as the "huff" leaped out, to burn a hole in the beams above. One could mark the little light of the slow matches at those guns where the flints of the locks had broken. One could see a sailor's face in the glow as he blew at the red end to clear away the ashes.

The least pleasant part of a ship of war in action was the waist or midship part, near the main rigging. It was the custom in these sea engagements to converge a broadside fire upon some central point in the opposing ship's side. The men stationed in the waist or main battery always suffered more in proportion than the men at the after or forward guns. That part of a ship's lower-deck between the fore and after hatchways, was known as "the slaughter-house," on account of the massacre which generally took place at that part. In the midst of the fury and confusion, with the ship shaking like a tautened rope from the concussion, and the blood "flowing like bilge water," there was yet a certain order and human purpose. The lieutenants walked to and fro about the batteries, regulating the fire, and keeping the men to their guns. The powder-boys skipped here and there on their errands for powder. The half-dozen men told off for cockpit duty came and went with the wounded, or paused at the gun-ports to heave a dead or dying man overboard, "with no other ceremony than shoving him through the port." Now and then some men left their guns and ran on deck to do any sail-trimming which might be necessary. Others broke away to bring up shot from the hold. If the ship carried any women or sailors' wives they, too, were employed about the deck in carrying water or powder. The master-at-arms went his rounds slowly, passing from deck to deck, asking for complaints, and noting how things were going. He had to make a note of the losses at the guns, of the expenditure of powder, and of the shot-holes between wind and water. His visits were godsends to the men working below the gun-deck in the magazines. The work there was mechanical, not feverish, like the work of the men at the guns. They had time to think, and found the situation "not one of danger, but most wounding of the feelings, and trying to the patience." One of the gunner's crew of H.M.S. *Goliath,* a 74-gun ship engaged at the battle of St Vincent, has told us that—

"I was stationed in the after-magazine serving powder from the screen, and could see nothing; but I could feel every shot that struck the *Goliath;* and the cries and groans of the wounded were most distressing, as there was only the thickness of the blankets of the screen between me and them. Busy as I was, the time hung upon me with a dreary weight. Not a soul spoke to me but the master-at-arms, as he went his rounds to inquire if all was safe. No sick person ever longed more for his physician than I for the voice of the master-at-arms. I would, if I had had my choice, have been on the deck; there I would have seen what was passing, and the time would not have hung so heavy."

If, during the engagement, the ships came grinding together, with a crash which knocked the lower-deck ports in, the matter was settled by boarding. The two or three men of each gun's crew who were told off as boarders were then "called away." They dropped their gun-tackles, drew their cutlasses and pistols, and skipped up on deck, into the enemy's rigging, and down on to her decks, to carry her by hand-to-hand fighting. more generally the action was determined by superior gunnery. The ship which lost her rudder or her foremast, or caught fire either aloft or below, was the one to strike. If one of the combatants became unmanageable her opponent took up a position on her bow or quarter, and raked her into submission, at a safe distance. When a ship struck a boat was sent to take possession of her. Her officers were sent aboard the captor as the guests of the ward-room and cabin. The men were hunted down into the hold under a guard of marines. If they showed signs of rising, or if they were too numerous for safety, they were put in irons. In extreme cases they were battened down below, with cannon, loaded with grape, pointing down the hatchways at them.

We quote part of the account of a boy who fought in one of the hottest of our frigate actions. The action belongs to a period half-a-dozen years after that of Trafalgar, but nevertheless, as the author says, "it will reveal the horrors of war, and show at what a fearful price a victory is won or lost."

"The whole scene grew indescribably confused and horrible. I was busily supplying my gun with powder, when I saw blood suddenly fly from the arm of a man stationed at our gun. I saw nothing strike him; the effect alone was visible.....the third lieutenant tied his handkerchief round the wounded arm, and sent the groaning wretch below to the surgeon. The cries of the wounded rang through all parts of the ship....those more fortunate men who were killed outright were immediately thrown overboard..... Two of the boys stationed on the quarter-deck were killed. A man, who saw one of them killed, afterwards told me that his powder caught fire and burnt the flesh almost off his face. In this pitiable situation, the agonised boy lifted up both hands, as if imploring relief, when a passing shot instantly cut him in two.....A man named Aldrich had one of his hands cut off by a shot, and almost at the same moment he received another shot, which tore open his bowels in a terrible manner. As he fell, two or three men caught him in their arms and, as he could not live, threw him overboard..... Our men kept cheering with all their might. I cheered with them, though I confess I scarcely knew for what. Certainly there was nothing very inspiriting in the aspect of things where I was stationed. Not only had we several boys and men killed and wounded, but several of the guns were disabled. The one I belonged to had a piece of the muzzle knocked out.....The brave boatswain, who came from the sick-bay to the din of battle, was fastening a stopper on a backstay, which had been shot away, when his head was smashed to pieces by a cannon-ball; another man, going to complete the unfinished task, was also struck down.....A fellow named John, who for some petty offence had been sent on board as a punishment, was carried past me wounded. I distinctly heard the large blood drops fall pat, pat, pat on the deck. Even a poor goat kept by the officers for her milk did not escape the general carnage; her hind legs were shot off, and poor Nan was thrown overboard. Such was the terrible scene, amid which we kept on our shouting and firing. I felt pretty much as I suppose everyone does at such a time. We all appeared cheerful, but I know that many a serious thought ran through my mind.....I thought a great deal of the other world.....but being without any particular knowledge of religious truth I satisfied myself by repeating again and again the Lord's Prayer."

The poor little boy was barely fourteen years old.

After an action a supply of venegar was heated for the sprinkling of the ship, to drive away the smell of blood from decks and beams. The last of the dead were thrown overboard, the wounded were made as comfortable as the circumstance allowed, and as many men as could be spared were sent on deck to knot and splice the rigging.

Before the repairs were begun the cannon were secured, and a gill of rum served out to every man and boy. Then the heaviest work of the action began. "It is after the action the disagreeable part commences." There was then no excitement to support the worker. The tired men had to turn to with a will, to unbend sails and bend new ones, to send up new spars, or new yards, to reeve new running-rigging, and set up new stays and shrouds. "For days they have no remission of their toil, repairing the rigging and other parts injured in the action." The work of a prize-crew, in charge of a prize, was especially arduous, for they were generally a mere handful of men, barely sufficient to sail the vessel, let alone to repair her. A prize-crew were sometimes too busy to clean the prize's decks. The *Chesapeake* came into Halifax six days after her capture by the *Shannon* with her decks still horrible with blood, and with human fingers sticking in her sides, "as though they had been thrust through from without." In any case a ship which had been in a hot engagement needed to be cleansed in every part with vinegar, and disinfected with brimstone, before the shambles smell was removed from her.

The sailors were often inconvenienced indirectly during a hot engagement by the destruction of the hammocks. The hammock nettings stopped a great number of cannon balls, and the gangways were frequently littered with hammocks thrown out by the shot, torn in pieces, or shot clean through. As a 32lb. round shot made a very big hole in a purser's blanket, and as the sailors paid for their own bedding, this was a real hardship. However, "everything is a joke at sea." The thought of prize-money atoned for the discomfort.

Chapter VIII

The daily routine / Sunday / Ship visiting

The day of a man-of-war's man began at midnight, or at four in the morning, according to the alternation of the watches. If he had the middle-watch, from 12 p.m. till 4 a.m., he came on deck at midnight and remained there till 4 a.m., doing any duty which appeared necessary. The work at night in fine weather was easy. The men had but to trim the sails, and be ready for a call. The boatswain's mates, with a midshipman or two, kept watch on the forecastle. Look-outs were placed in the tops and cross-trees. The sentries, helmsmen, officer of the watch, midshipmen, and master's mates, went to their posts on the poop and quarter-deck. The remainder of the watch were supposed by the Articles of War to keep awake on pain of death. Some captains and lieutenants allowed those not actually on watch as look-out men to sleep during their night-watches, if the weather was very fine. The act of sleeping during a night-watch in the tropics was known as "taking a caulk," because by lying on the plank-seams the sailors' jackets were marked with lines of tar. In those ships aboard which the sailors were expected to keep awake, the boatswain's mates walked round with their starters, or kept buckets of water ready to wake anyone who fell asleep. In wet weather there was no sleeping in any ship during the night-watch on deck, because the men were put to collecting rain water for washing clothes. In foul weather they were too busily employed in other ways.

A few minutes before eight bells, or 4 a.m., the quarter-masters stole down the after-ladders to call the midshipmen, mates, and lieutenant of the other watch. The boatswain's mates took their pipes to the fore and main hatchways, and blew the prolonged shrill call "All Hands," following it up by a shout of "Starboard (or Larboard) Watch Ahoy. Rouse out there, you sleepers. Hey. Out or down here." At this order the watch below, who were snugly sleeping in their hammocks, turned out at once without waiting till they were properly awake. When they had turned out they put on their clothes (if they had taken them off) and bustled up on deck with the starters after them. At eight bells they were mustered, and sent to their stations. The wheel and look-outs were relieved. The log was hove, and the rate of sailing marked on the board. The men of the other watch, who had kept the deck since midnight, were then allowed to go below to their hammocks.

Shortly after four o'clock the idlers were called up. The cook lit his fires in the

Published at Ackermann Gallery 101 Strand London Aug 13.1803.

The VETERAN's ADDRESS to a YOUNG SAILOR.

YOU are now, young Man, entering on a scene of life the most glorious and enterprising—that of an ENGLISH SAILOR; to you is, in part, delegated the care of the British Empire: be mindful of the sacred trust you have in charge; be watchful as the lynx in the hour of danger, and pour the thunder of your cannon on the insulting Foes of ALBION; then shall the spirit of immortal HAWKE animate your bosom, and the shades of departed Heroes lead you on to VICTORY! An imperious and daring Invader threatens to approach your shores; but tell him, with a Stentor's voice, that BRITONS never will stoop to Slavery! BRITANNIA, seated on her chalky Cliffs, smiles at his threats and arrogant presumption. Bring to his mind the deeds of mighty DRAKE, when SPAIN's ARMADA shrunk beneath his valour; let HOWARD, BLAKE, and POCOCK, (deathless names!) make the Invader tremble; RUSSEL, BOSCAWEN, and a train of Heroes fill the glorious list. Be these your great examples in the hour of battle; or, if more modern deeds excite your ardour, think on the fearless DUNCAN, brave CORNWALLIS, HOWE, WARREN, HOOD, the famed ST. VINCENT, and the undaunted HERO OF THE NILE! names that will ever live in Time's eternal calendar! With such examples, GLORY must attend you, and your grateful Country shall reward your gallant prowess. Again remember the important charge you have in trust. Farewell! be vigilant, be bold—true to your GOD, your COUNTRY, and your KING!

Plate 12 *Recruiting propaganda of the period.*

Plate 13 *(a) Equity, or a sailor's prayers before Trafalgar — a Dublin print of the period.
(b) Mess deck scene on the Victory. There were usually four to eight sailors in a mess.*

galley, and began to boil the abominable burgoo for breakfast. The carpenter and carpenter's mates came on deck and began their work. The boatswain came up, and the watch on deck began active duty. Before 5 a.m. the watch took off their shoes and stockings, rolled up their trousers to the thigh, rigged the pumps, got out the scrubbers and buckets, and began to wash her down. First of all the decks were wetted by means of the head-pump and buckets. After the bucket men came a couple of hands sprinkling sand on the wetted planks. When the sand had been sprinkled the main body of the seamen took their holystones, and went upon their hands and knees to whiten the deck to its usual spotless whiteness. The gangways and main-deck could be holystoned by a large stone, a block of holystone weighing many pounds, with rings at each end. The sailors rove ropes through the rings, and ran the block to and fro on the wet and sanded planking. All the out-of-the-way places, under guns, carronade slides, bitts, etc. etc., were scrubbed by the handstones, or "prayer-books." It was hard, and often unpleasant, work, scrubbing the decks in all weathers, some fourteen hours after the last meal. The upper and main decks were thus whitened every morning. It was a real hardship to kneel for an hour or two on sanded planks, in frosty Channel weather. Many sailors developed sore knees from the practice.

After the holystoners came the broom and bucket men, who swilled and swept the dirty sand into the waterways, and so overboard through the scuppers. After these came the swabbers, who flogged the damp decks with swabs till they had dried them. The little brasswork about the rails and bitts was then brightened. The ropes were coiled, flaked, or flemished down, and the wash-deck gear, of holystones, buckets and brooms, was returned to the lockers and hooks. By seven o'clock the work was practically finished, and the decks nearly dry. The first lieutenant came on deck at about this time to begin his long day's supervision. At about half-past seven the boatswain's mates went below to the berth-deck and piped "All hands. Up hammocks," a pipe which brought up the sleepers and filled the decks with scurrying figures carrying their lashed-up hammocks to the nettings, where they were stowed in order by the quarter-masters and midshipmen. By 8 a.m. the captain had come on deck, the last of the hammocks had been stowed, the mess tables had been lowered into position between the guns, and the cook had wreaked his worst upon the burgoo, or Scotch coffee. At a word from the captain the boatswain piped to breakfast, eight bells was struck upon the ship's bell, and nearly every man except the helmsman, lookout men, and officers on duty, slipped down to breakfast. Half-an-hour was allowed for this meal on weekdays. At half-past eight the watch was called, and those who had slept from 4 till 7.30 a.m. came upon deck, bringing with them the bags and chests from the berths. These were stowed on the booms, while the lower deck was cleaned (by the watch below) with the dry holystone and sand. The lower-deck was never washed down with water save in fine, dry weather, when the ports could be opened, and port-fires burned to dry the wet planking. At other times it was sanded, scraped and holystoned, then swept with dry brooms, and perhaps swabbed over. The lower-deck beams were often sponged over with vinegar as a disinfectant.

The cooks of the different messes passed the forenoon watch in cooking in the galley, cleaning up the mess utensils, and getting dinner ready. Those who had the watch below were often free to do as they wished.[1] They could sleep, or yarn, or mend their clothes. Their hammocks were stowed in the nettings, but if lucky they could sleep in between the guns, on the bare deck, provided the space was not wanted by one of the ship's artificers, such as the carpenter. Those who had the watch on deck were employed in the work of the ship, in the rigging, or about the guns, doing the never-finished duties of sailormen. Some captains preferred to send their watch below to exercise at the guns directly they had cleaned the lower-deck. At six bells, or eleven o'clock, the captain, who had finished breakfast, seen the young gentlemen's logs, examined the boatswain's, purser's, and carpenter's accounts, and had a talk with the first lieutenant, came on deck with the black list, and called all hands to witness punishment. The master-at-arms brought up his men in irons from the bilboes under the half-deck. The gratings were rigged, the hands mustered, and the poor fellows flogged according to the captain's pleasure and the Articles of War. By the time the execution had been done and the blood swabbed up it was time to take the sun's altitude. The master, master's mates, and midshipmen brought out their sextants and quadrants. Noon was reported when the sun reached the meridian. The clock was put back or put forward; eight bells was struck; the boatswain's mate piped his long, cheery "pipe to dinner," all hands ran below with a song, and then began "the pleasantest part of the day." Dinner generally took about half-an-hour, from twelve till half-past. It was a merry meal, eaten cheerily, with a great buzz of talk all along the gun-deck. At half-past twelve there came a great clink of cans and banging of tin plates on the tables. The fifer took his flute to the main or upper deck, where the master's mate stood by the tub to dispense sea ambrosia to the ship's company. At the sound of one bell the fifer struck up "Nancy Dawson," or some other lively tune, such as "Drops of Brandy," and immediately the ship's company took up the tune. The mess cooks seized their black-jacks and hurried to the tub where the grog was served out. They then carried it below to the messes, where it was drunken down, with many songs and toasts. The debts were discharged, bets settled, and purchases effected. Grog time was the one happy hour of the day. With grog and an occasional battle a sailor was almost contented.

At half-past one o'clock, when the last oozings of the black jack had been drained, the watch on deck was called to duty. The watch below were sometimes allowed to keep below, to sleep if they could, or to amuse themselves as they pleased, as soon as they had swept away the crumbs of dinner. More frequently they were called on deck with the rest, to be drilled into smartness. Top-sails were reefed, and upper spars sent down, the ship was tacked and wore, the fire bell was rung, the men were sent to stations for letting go anchor. Landsmen and raw hands were taken below by the gunner's mates, and trained at the heavy guns. Other squads were drilled in the use of the musket or cutlass. Boarding parties were stationed at their respective guns and suddenly called

1 *As soon as the lower deck had been cleaned.*

away, when they were expected to snatch up pistols, cutlasses, and boarding pikes, and to run on deck to hack the air furiously beside the hammock nettings. Some captains who drilled the crew thus allowed their complements to take an occasional afternoon watch below, especially in heavy weather. Once or twice on each cruise they turned them up in the afternoon "to dance and skylark," with the ship's fiddler to play their dance tunes. At 4 p.m. the boatswain piped to supper, which lasted half-an-hour, and was made pleasant by the second serving out of grog. Shortly after supper, but before sunset, the drummer beat to quarters. All hands had to repair to their stations. The guns were cast loose. The midshipmen and lieutenants had to make a minute inspection of the men and gun gear. The pumps were rigged, the lifebuoys were placed in position, and the ship reported to the captain as being in good order. It was at this evening muster that the master-at-arms made most of his arrests. Many poor fellows, who had saved up their dinner grog and taken a "long swig at the halliards" before quarters, were then put in irons for the next day's black list. A little thickness or gaiety in the voice, or a little unsteadiness in the walk, was always inquired into. He was a happy sailor who had the first watch below and a head so strong that nothing showed till a couple of hours after taking.

When the company had finished their exercise and secured the guns for the night it was time for the hammocks to be piped down. The men ran on deck, received their hammocks from the nettings, slung them in their places, and then stood by till eight bells. At eight o'clock the first night-watch was called and set, and the watch below went down to their hammocks until midnight. The lights were extinguished, or covered over, so that they would not show from a distance. The master-at-arms, or ship's corporals, began their policeman's rounds. The first lieutenant turned in for the night. Quiet settled down upon the ship to be broken only by the creaking of the tiller-ropes, the patting of the reef-points, and the occasional "All's Well" cry of the sentries, showing that they had not fallen asleep.

The watch and watch system, four hours on and four hours off, with the four hours off constantly broken in upon by the ship's routine, was severe and harassing. It meant that the sailor had but four hours of sleep one night, and a bare seven hours' the night following. The little naps they managed to take in the forenoons and afternoons were hardly worth mentioning; they were too uncertain, too liable to interruption. Even in their watches below at night they were liable to be called on deck to tack, to wear, to shorten sail, or to go to their stations. Once a month, at least, they were drummed up to general quarters in the middle of their dreams. Every Thursday the hammocks were called up at 4 a.m., and the morning-watch was passed by the men in washing clothes. Every Monday the day-watches were fully occupied by gun drill, target practice, and musket exercise. Every Thursday afternoon all hands were sent to mend their clothes. They were at all times liable to be called upon for works of supererogation, such as sweeping or coiling down.

On Saturdays the men slung clean hammocks. They passed the afternoon in holy-stoning the decks, ready for Sunday, as the daily routine on Sunday was always rather lighter than on week-days. The Saturday cleaning made it unnecessary to holystone the decks on Sunday morning. The men merely sprinkled the planks and swabbed them down, instead of scrubbing them. The hammocks were piped up half-an-hour earlier than usual, and stowed with more than usual care, "numbers out," so that the clean white cloths made a brave show all down the nettings. Breakfast was piped half-an-hour earlier than usual, so that the forenoon-watch should be long enough both for divisions and Divine Service. While breakfast was in progress, the boatswain's mates passed the word for the company to shave and put on clean shirts, before coming on deck, and the gun-decks were swiftly dry-holystoned, and carefully swept by the ship's sweepers. Every scrap of dust and dirt was removed. The rags and brick-dust for the polishing of the little bright work in the ships were brought out, and used till the brass and steel were shining like gold. The cook polished his coppers. The armourer put a shine upon his cutlasses, muskets, and pistols. The cooper got his casks in order. The boatswain, sailmaker, carpenter, and purser saw to the ordering of their respective store-rooms. The quarter-gunners made the round of their guns, and in fine weather traversed them, in order to clean the plank covered by the carriages, and to remove any shakings or mess clouts stowed beneath them by idle sweepers. The gunner down in the magazine saw that the sea cocks which flooded the magazine in case of fire were ready for use, that the right proportion of cartridges was filled, and that the bands of the copper-bound powder casks were polished, with a little soft rag. Every petty officer and man aboard was busy polishing, cleaning, and arranging. The time for preparation was limited. Much had to be done, yet two hours and a half, at most, was the time allowed for the duty. Before half-past ten the men contrived to "shave and shift" themselves, using the head and forecastle and the berths between the guns for their toilet-rooms. The barbers plied their business in the head, while all about the forward parts of the ship one might have seen the old sailors, sitting on inverted mess kids, having their queues dressed by their mates. Others feverishly mended their shirts and trousers, curled their ringlets, cleaned their shoes, or shaved their three-day beards.

A few minutes before half-past ten the sweepers again took their brooms over the speckless decks, while the first lieutenant made a hurried examination of the whole ship, to see that nothing was amiss. Then, at half-past ten, the bell struck, and the drummer took his drum and beat to muster. The men, in their clean blue trousers and white shirts, or clean white trousers and blue shirts, fell in on the gangways, main-deck, and quarter-deck. The ship's boys fell in on the fore-castle. When they had all fallen in, with their toes on an indicated seam or line of tar, the midshipmen called them over. The lieutenants then inspected them, to send down any man improperly or dirtily dressed. The surgeon took the opportunity to examine the men for traces of scurvy. After these preliminary examinations the captain came round to inspect the men, and to receive the reports of the junior officers. The captain then examined every part of the ship, from the forecastle to the lower hold. He was accompanied on his rounds by the first lieutenant, to whom he made any necessary complaint. The lower parts of the ship were lighted up during the inspection by the petty and warrant officers in charge of them. It was the custom of many officers to wear a white glove while going round the ship, so that a light touch inside a cook's copper, or on a beam, would betray the presence of any dirt or dust.

As soon as the inspection had come to an end the sailors were released from the misery of toeing the deck seam, and driven aft to Divine Service,[1] which was held on the quarter-deck, in the open air. They sat on buckets and mess kids, and on inverted match tubs, or on the slides of the after-carronades. A bell was tolled to call them aft, and a "church pendant" was hoisted at the peak as soon as they were in their places. The chaplain then came forward to the after-hatchway gratings, and read the prayers prescribed by the Liturgy, afterwards giving a short address. If there were no chaplain the captain was expected to officiate, but the captains generally got out of the difficulty by reading the Articles of War. After church the men were piped to dinner. They were then free (as far as the work of the ship allowed it) to do as they wished till supper time, at four or four-thirty. The free Sunday afternoons were passed in rest and quietness on the various decks. The watch on deck slept on the forecastle, or walked to and fro on the gangways, or spun their yarns between the forward-carronades. The watch below generally kept on the lower-deck, or on one side of the main-deck (the other being reserved for a promenade for the lieutenants). They formed into little parties between the guns, at the mess tables, where they yarned, or read, or played chequers (draughts) for the afternoon. Some slept on the deck, with a rolled-up coat for a pillow. Others stole away to some quiet nook, where they could "rattle the bones," using their tarry fists for dice-boxes. Cards and dice were forbidden, but the ships were manned so indiscriminately that every complement contained card-sharpers, gamblers, and professional rooks. These men indulged in their favourite games, keeping a smart look-out for the master-at-arms and ship's corporal.

In port and in the fleets at sea it was the custom to allow "ship visiting" on Sunday afternoons if the weather were fine. The sailors were not allowed to go ashore, save in exceptional circumstances; but to make amends for this restriction they were allowed to visit the other ships of war in company. The boats were kept busy all the afternoon conveying the "liberty men" from one ship to the other. It seems that the ships vied with each other in hospitality; many of the men being well content to give up half their Sunday grog if, by doing so, they might make their visitors drunk. "Ship visiting" was subversive of all good discipline, though in conception it was humane, and kindly meant. The men often got very drunk, and often quarrelled with their hosts. If they agreed with their hosts they returned to their own ships discontented, and eager to find fault with their officers and shipmates.

After supper on Sundays the weekly muster was held, at which the men had to pass one by one before the captain to answer to their names. After muster, when the drunken men had been secured, the drummer beat to quarters; the guns were examined

---

1 *Edward Thompson says: "You will find some little outward appearance of religion and Sunday prayers, but the congregation is generally driven together by the boatswain, who neither spares oaths nor blows."*

and pronounced to be fit for action; the hammocks were piped down, and the first watch was set. After the setting of the watch the day was accounted over. The lights were extinguished, and the watch below turned in. The ordinary routine of the ship was again imposed upon all hands.

Chapter IX

In port / Jews / Lovely Nan / Mutinies / Their punishment /
Sailor songs / "Drops of Brandy" / "Spanish Ladies," etc. /
Flags / Salutes

When a ship came into port after a long absence at sea or on a foreign station, with several years of pay due to her crew, she was surrounded by boats from the shore containing "Girls and Jews." During the wars the sailors were given hardly any shore leave, lest they should run away. Those who did get ashore were so watched by the land folk eager to earn a little head or blood money—the reward for capturing a deserter—that they had little pleasure in their jaunts on land. They never touched their pay till the ship was about to sail again, so that they had small chance of enjoying themselves, or of buying necessaries if they did succeed in getting out of the ship. The Jews knew this very well, and therefore plied a very thriving business with the sailors at every great sea-port. When the ship came to an anchor they came off in their wherries with all manner of fancy articles such as the sailors cared for. "Gold" watches, which ticked very loudly, and went for a week, made a very profitable line. Gold seals, of the same quality; bright brass telescopes, which put an edge of brilliant colours round everything one saw through them; scarlet and blue silk handkerchiefs, fancy shoes, shoe-buckles, suspenders, watch-chains, diamond rings, etc.—all of these things were laid out, with a great deal of glitter, on the pedlar's tray amidships. For all this trash they asked enormous prices, about five times more than the things were worth. Others brought sailor's clothes, of cuts and colours more beautiful than those sold by the purser, such as blue-and-white striped trousers, as baggy as the mouths of wind-sails, waistcoats like tropical sunsets, and neckerchiefs like blood and broken eggs. Others brought little natty straw hats, with ribbons neatly painted with the name of the ship, or glazed tarpaulin hats with linings of some violently-coloured cloth. Some brought sailor's necessaries, such as gaudy crockery, clay pipes, "silver" tobacco stoppers, clasp and sheath knives, real silver spoons, hammock stretchers, tin pots and pans, boxes of sugar, red-herrings, eggs Dutch cheeses, butter, apples, onions, etc. Nearly all of them had skins and bladders full of red-eye, gin or similar "Sailor's joy," such as would give a waister the action of a port-admiral. Towards the end of the long French wars the captains grew more strict in their admission of these creatures. They allowed them aboard only under certain conditions, generally restricting them to the quarter-deck and gangways, where they did business under the eyes of the officers and the marine sentries. This kept them from smuggling drink aboard in any quantity, though they generally contrived to smuggle in a little, despite the searching of the master-at-arms. It also kept them from cheating the sailors unduly, and from being cheated or man-handled by the sailor's ladies. Another regulation adopted towards the end of the war kept the Jews out of the ship till pay-day, a day or two before the ship sailed again. In the eighteenth century they came aboard directly the ship was anchored, for in addition to the slop and bumboat trade they carried on the profitable business of money-lending, advancing ready money, at a ruinous rate of interest, on the sailors' pay-tickets. The sailors knew very well that the Jews cheated them, but they had no alternative but to submit. In the matter of slops and trinkets they were cheated less badly than over the pay, for when they came to hand over the money for the gear they had bought they were generally drunk with "the parting cans." In this condition they argued and wrangled, and blacked the Jews' eyes, and flung the pedlars' trays down the hatches, and often enough refused to pay a red cent of the money claimed. However, as Marryat says, "the Jews' charges were so extravagant that if one-third of their bills were paid there still remained a profit." When the strangers were turned out of the ship on pay-day nights there were some lively scenes between the sergeant of marines, or the master-at-arms, and the sailors and Jews who felt themselves cheated.

In the old days, when a man-of-war came into a home port, the boatmen on the along-shore made their bargains with the women of the town. They charged each woman several shillings for the trip out to the ship, the women stipulating that if they failed to please the sailors the fare should not be paid. This stipulation made the boatmen very careful what women they took with them. They rowed out only the prettiest and the best-dressed, for if the women were not chosen by the sailors they lost their fare, and had all their trouble for nothing. Besides, the lieutenants were very jealous of the reputations of their ships. It was not unusual for a lieutenant to overlook the boatloads as they came alongside, and to refuse to admit any ugly women, or any woman not smartly attired or freshly painted. When the boats came alongside, each man slipped down the gangway, made his choice, and carried her down to the berth. We would add that most of the sailors were young men, that they sometimes stayed several years away from England without so much as seeing a woman, and that a lower-deck, at that time, was neither refined nor prudish.

A woman so chosen remained aboard with her chooser, or with any other man whom she preferred. The protector, or fancy-man, kept her with him while the ship remained in port, sharing his allowance with her, and buying her little delicacies from the bumboats which came alongside. A man-of-war of the first-rate had frequently 500 women aboard at the same time, each woman being ready to swear that she was the lawful wife of her protector. With the women came drink, and what with the drink and the women the ship's discipline came to a stop. The master-at-arms searched every woman who came aboard, for bladders full of spirits, scent-bottles, etc. etc. Marines kept guard on the chains overlooking the ship's sides, so that no drink should be conveyed through the ports from shore boats. The head ports were barred in. The sentries guarded the forecastle, so that no man might lower a bucket privily over the bows. Every boat which

92

came alongside was searched by the ship's corporals. Every boatman who came aboard was examined and felt. But, with all these precautions, the red-eye came aboard. Nothing kept it out very long. It came aboard a little at a time, inside cocoa-nuts, balls of lard, oranges, or anything with tolerable cubic capacity. When it had come aboard the lower-deck became a pandemonium. The men and women drank and quarrelled between the guns. The decks were allowed to become dirty. Drunken sailors could be found lying under each hatchway. Drunken women were continually coming aft to insult the officers, or to lodge a complaint outside a lieutenant's province. Sometimes the women ran aloft to wave their petticoats to the flagship. Now and then they fell from aloft while performing this manoeuvre, and so broke their necks and came to an unhappy end.

In some ways they may have been of benefit to the sailors. Though they cheated them themselves they kept others from cheating them. They were not without tenderness, nor were they so unfaithful as most people would suppose. In many cases the sailors married them. In others, the women grew so fond of their protectors that they followed the ship by land, if she were ordered, say, from Spithead to Sheerness, or to some other home port. It was not unusual for a monstrous regiment of women to march right across England so that they might join their mates on the other side.

When a ship set sail after a long sojourn in a home port there was a great deal of misery upon the lower-deck. The sailors, or at anyrate the tender-hearted ones, were melancholy; the women were either crying or drunk; the Jews were clamouring for their moneys; the bumboat people wanted their bills paid; and the sailors were drinking parting cans and hoping to pay their debts with a loose fore-topsail. Before the marines drove the women out of the ship the tender-hearted sailors came aft to the captain for permission to take their wives to sea with them. A line-of-battle ship often carried as many as a dozen women to sea. It seems that the practice did not die out for many years after the time of which we write. Some admirals strictly forbade it, as fatal to all discipline. As a rule, however, the married warrant officers, and perhaps a few men, obtained leave to take their wives with them, on the understanding that misconduct would involve their instant dismissal. A captain had to weigh such applications very carefully, admitting only the most respectable of those who offered. He had also to suffer patiently the abuses and menaces of the harridans he refused to ship.

The partings between the robuster sailors and their ladies were not marked by any great flow of sentiment. The women smuggled off a last bladder of red-eye for the brewing of a good-bye flip. The sailors bought onions and turnips, the latter as a symbol of subsequent unfaithfulness, the former to induce tears in "eyes unus'd to flow." With a good deal of merry, black-guardly banter, a good deal of drunken squabble, and a very energetic wrangle over the sailors' money, the last day aboard came to an end. Before sunset of the day before sailing the strangers were driven out of the ship, and bundled down into the shore boats. The drunken men were lashed into their hammocks till morning, when discipline again took hold and reduced them to order.

After a spell in port a ship was nearly always dirty and evil-smelling. The men were diseased, and in poor condition. It generally took a month to bring them back to their old standard of smartness. Very few of them came to sea with any money. The little left to them after they had cashed their tickets, or swept the heaps of coins into their hats, had gone to their women, or to the Jews. After the wars our roads were thronged with sturdy beggars, who had been in the King's ships, and had wasted their substance in the home ports. It is said that the number of loose women in Portsmouth decreased at that time from 20,000 to about a fifth of that number.

The custom of admitting women to the ships was not abolished for many years—barely more than sixty years ago. In the early forties, the captain of a frigate in the West Indies sent ashore for 300 women, so that every man and boy aboard might have a black mistress during their stay in the port. A white planter supplied the women from his plantations. The lieutenants were not allowed to keep women on board, but until the beginning of the nineteenth century the midshipmen, and some of the junior ward-room officers, indulged as licentiously, with as little authoritative restraint, as their inferiors. An old naval surgeon, writing in 1826, tells us that he knew of several fine lads who died miserably from perseverance "in their debauched habits." After the first decade of the nineteenth century the captains were more careful of the manners of the young gentlemen. Their vices, if practised at all, were then practised ashore, out of the captain's jurisdiction. After 1814 the service was purged of some of its vicious officers by the examination known as "passing for a gentleman," to which we have alluded elsewhere.

The songs most popular among the sailors were not always those purporting to deal with life afloat. Their most popular song was a song very popular ashore. It is still well known, though the old name for it, "Drops of Brandy," is now nearly forgotten. The tune is an old country dance tune. The words the sailors sang to it are the familiar:

"And Johnny shall have a new bonnet
And Johnny shall go to the fair,
And Johnny shall have a blue ribbon
To tie up his bonny brown hair.
And why should I not love Johnny
And why should not Johnny love me,
And why should I not love Johnny
As well as another bodie."

The tune is simple and beautiful. When the marines and waisters manned the capstan, to weigh the anchor, aboard one of these old ships of war the pipers struck up "Drops of Brandy," to put a heart into the jollies as they hove around. It was sung by many merry sailors over their grog, in the dark sea snuggeries between the guns. A tune which kept many a miserable pressed man from going over the side should be reverently treated We give the music below.

94

Drops of Brandy Campbell's Dances, Book 11ᵗʰ, circa 1800

The tune the fifers played to call the sailors to the grog tub was "Nancy Dawson," a tune well known to everyone as "Sally in our Alley." The "double double double beat," which drummed the men to quarters, is also well known, as "Hearts of Oak"— a song still popular in many parts of England. After these, the best-known song was that known as "Spanish Ladies," a beautiful old song, long popular at sea, and still familiar to many people. It has been quoted so often, by so many popular writers, that we must apologise for reprinting it. It is still sung at sea, especially aboard American merchant-vessels. The Americans sing it with various alterations.

Spanish Ladies

arranged by Martin Shaw

95

SPANISH LADIES

Farewell and adieu to you fine Spanish Ladies—
  Farewell and adieu all you Ladies of Spain—
For we've received orders to sail for Old England
  And perhaps we shall never more see you again.

Chorus— We'll rant and we'll roar like true British Sailors,
        We'll range and we'll roam over all the salt seas,
        Until we strike soundings in the Channel of Old England—
        From Ushant to Scilly 'tis thirty-five leagues.

We hove our ship to when the wind was sou'west, boys,
  We hove our ship to for to strike soundings clear,
Then we filled our main-tops'l and bore right away, boys,
  And right up the Channel our course we did steer.
*Chorus—*We'll rant and we'll roar, etc.

The first land we made it is known as the Deadman,
  Next Ram Head near Plymouth, Start, Portland, and Wight;
We sailed past Beachy, past Fairley and Dungeness,
  And then bore away for the South Foreland Light.
*Chorus—*We'll rant and we'll roar, etc.

Then the signal was made for the grand fleet to anchor
  All all in the Downs that night for to meet,
So stand by your stoppers, see clear your shank-painters,
  Haul all your clew-garnets, stick out tacks and sheets
*Chorus—*We'll rant and we'll roar, etc.

Now let every man toss off a full bumper,
  Now let every man toss off a full bowl,
For we will be jolly and drown melancholy
  In a health to each jovial and true-hearted soul.
*Chorus—*We'll rant and we'll roar, etc.

Many of Charles Dibdin's songs were popular in our fleets and naval hospitals. His most popular song appears to have been "Tom Bowling," a song which seems to have continued in the popular favour until our own time. His songs sent so many young men to the Tower tender as naval recruits that the Government pensioned him.

It was hardly possible for human beings to live contentedly under the iron regulations of a man-of-war. One has but to read the books left to us by the sailors to realise the peculiar horror of the life between-decks. Cooped up there, like sardines in a tin, were several hundreds of men, gathered by force and kept together by brutality. A lower-deck was the home of every vice, every baseness, and every misery. The life lived there was something like the life of the negro slave who happened to be housed in a gaol. It is not strange that the men sometimes revolted, and broke out in open mutiny in order to obtain redress. The story of the mutiny of the Bounty, in which the men were "hazed" into turning their obnoxious officers adrift in an open boat, is well known. The stories of the mutinies at the Nore and at Spithead are also familiar. The seamen concerned in these latter mutinies have been held up for execration, but we would ask the indignant reader to learn something of the sufferings which prompted them, and of the temperate and manly way in which they made their wants known. They asked for a slight increase of pay, amounting to about three-pence a day for each man, so that they might be able to support their wives and families. They asked for an occasional day ashore; for fresh vegetables when in port, for better food, and for more humane treatment for their wounded. They also asked that they might be paid in cash instead of by ticket, and that the pay of the wounded might not be stopped while they lay in their hammocks under the surgeon's hands. They had suffered much from the treatment of some of their officers, but their attitude towards these men was singularly humane. They towed one brutal lieutenant ashore on a grating, and they very nearly hanged a marine officer for firing on a boat-load of delegates. With these exceptions they acted throughout with a moderation as praiseworthy as it was astonishing. They were less temperate aboard H.M.S. *Hermione,* a 32-gun frigate, commanded by Captain Hugh Pigot, the son of an admiral. Captain Pigot was one of the most tyrannical and cruel officers who ever held command. He maddened his crew by repeated acts of cruelty, which culminated at last off the South American coast. One quiet afternoon he drilled his topmen at reefing top-sails. While the men were doing their best, "lighting out," and "passing earrings," he called out to the men on the mizzen top-sail-yard that he would flog the last man down. In their hurry down from aloft two of the men fell on to the deck at the captain's feet, breaking all the bones in their bodies. His remark on this occasion was: "Heave those lubbers overboard!" That night the crew rose in open mutiny. They broke into the cabin, and stabbed Captain Pigot with repeated stabs, so that he died. They killed a number of the lesser officers, and turned several others adrift in a boat. They then sailed the *Hermione* into La Guayra, and handed her over to the Spanish authorities. She was captured in Puerto Cabello a couple of years later, by the boats of H.M.S. *Surprise.* Many of the mutineers were afterwards apprehended, and hanged.

Hanging was the usual end of a mutineer. Mutiny, being the one unpardonable sin in a sailor, was treated with far less mercy than desertion, or attempted desertion. The mutiny at the Nore[1] sent a considerable number of sailors to the yard-arm, and lesser

---

1 *The mutiny at Spithead—a far more serious matter than the mutiny at the Nore—was managed with such skill, and such temperance, that the King extended his pardon to the ringleaders. At the Nore the sailors were thought to have been the tools of the Radical party, and an example was made of Parker and his accomplices.*

mutinies were no less severely punished. A man who struck an officer was fairly certain to be hanged or flogged through the fleet. A man who raised a disturbance or headed an open rebellion, however trivial, was certain to be put to death. On one ship some sailors were taken in the act of violating the Twenty-Ninth Article of War. They were condemned to be punished publicly. Their shipmates, eager for the honour of the ship, begged that the sentence might not be carried out, less the crew should be hooted at throughout the fleet. On their request being refused, they at once broke out into a noisy disturbance on the lower-deck. Their officers ran down and secured the ringleaders, drove the remainder on deck, and promptly courtmartialled and hanged the offenders. At the cessation of hostilities in 1802 many of the sailors were dissatisfied with the orders relating to paying-off. Some ships stationed in the west were ordered to be paid off in London. Others were ordered off on some short cruise, which kept the sailors from joining the many merchant-ships then fitting out after the winter in port. The ringleaders of these little mutinies were hanged, though the occasion surely warranted a slighter punishment.

Many of our sailors deserted to the French, Spanish, and American services, where the routine was a little less severe, and the pay no worse. Those who were taken in foreign ships of war were invariably hanged at the fore yard-arm.

We have mentioned the narrow pendant, the long banner, with a red St George's cross on a white ground, and long red swallow-tail, which captains hoisted at the main-topgallant masthead, on placing a ship in commission. We now add a few words about some of the other flags and colours in use in the navy. The Royal Standard, which need not be described, was worn at the main-topgallant masthead of those ships which carried a member of the Royal Family. A ship which carried the Lord High Admiral or his Commissioners flew the Admiralty flag (a square red flag, with a golden anchor and cable in its centre) at the same place. An admiral of the fleet flew the Union Jack at the main-topgallant masthead of his own ship. An admiral of the white, or vice-admiral, flew the St George's banner at his fore-topgallant masthead. An admiral of the blue, or rear-admiral, flew a square blue flag at his mizzen-topgallant masthead. A commodore, or senior captain of the first class, flew a broad red swallow-tailed pendant at his main-topgallant masthead. If another commodore senior to him were in company he flew a white broad pendant marked with a red St George's cross. A commodore of the second class flew a blue broad pendant, unless a senior captain were sailing in company.

All ships in commission wore a red, white or blue ensign at the mizzen peak, according to the flag of the admiral under whom they sailed. They also carried a small Union Jack at the end of the bowsprit on a flagstaff above the spritsail-yard.

Flag officers had certain distinctive boat flags which they flew in the bows of their boats when they pulled ashore. There were also a number of coloured flags and pendants in use for signalling. The Union Jack was also used for signalling on certain important occasions such as the holding of a court-martial.

The Royal Standard, Admiralty flag, admirals' flags, and commodores' broad pendants were entitled to salutes of guns, varying in number from twenty-one guns (in the case of the first named) to nine (in the case of a second-class commodore). The numbers of guns fired in salute were always odd, following an ancient custom, not now explicable. Ambassadors consuls, foreign governors, and dukes were also saluted by guns. A salute was fired quickly, with an interval of about six seconds between each gun.

Merchant-ships, both English and foreign, were expected to lower their top-sails, or to let fly their topgallant sheets, when passing a British man-of-war. This old custom is now nearly obsolete, but the present writer has seen the master of a schooner lowering his top-sail in salute to a cruiser.

If it be the lot of the dead to pass, unviewed, along the streets of cities, or by the country hedgerows, conscious of the life about them, there is, surely, a prospective triumph for the beaten and the broken folk whose blood and agony have made easy, if indirectly, the passage of later pilgrims. Could the countless unselfish ones, the sufferers, "the great despisers," who bore so many miseries, that we, their descendants, might pass gaudy and comfortable days—could they but know how golden a thing their misery purchased, the memory of the old torture and the old injustice would be soothing and gentle like a charity.

In the years of which I have tried to write there were thousands upon thousands of sailors, wandering over many seas, in countless ships, standing their watches, doing the day's work, breaking their hearts, and dying young, not because they liked it, not because they hoped for glory, but because much suffering had to be endured before man could learn to inflict less suffering on his fellows. We sit here quietly to-day in London—in that London which, as Nelson said, "exists by victories at sea." Our great ships go thrashing hither and yon, turbulent and terrible, like islands of living iron. Here, in London, are the world's merchants, richer than the merchants of Tyre, whose purple clothed the kings of the world. Aboard those ships are the English sailors, the finest men afloat, living cheerfully the lives they have chosen, under humane and just captains.

There is no London merchant telling over gold in his counting-house, no man-of-war's man standing his watch at sea, who does not owe his gold or his rights to the men who lived wretched days long ago aboard old wooden battleships, under martinets. In order that they might live as they live, what misery, what blood and tears, fell to the portions of those who went before making straight the paths! For every quiet hour here in London, for every merry day at sea, what hecatombs were necessary!

In order that our days might be pleasant, those thousands of long-dead sailors had to live and suffer. They passed rough days—living hard, working hard, and dying hard. In order that we might live in peace at home they were dragged, with blows and curses, from their homes. In order that we might walk erect among men they cringed before tyrants, and lost their manhood at the gangway. In order that we might live on the luxuries of the world, brought from the East and the West, things of great cost, wines,

Plate 14 *(a) John Bull taking a luncheon.*
(b) Sailors in argument.

Plate 15 *(a) A Staffordshire earthenware mug of about 1800.*
(b) A three handled china loving cup made by Copeland for the centenary of the Battle of Trafalgar in 1905, the year in which Masefield wrote "Sea Life in Nelson's Time."

and spices, they were content, those great despisers, to eat salt junk and drink stinking water. They passed, those mighty ones, in the blackness of the cockpit, in the roaring hell of the gun-deck, that we might hear no noise of battle. They were well pleased to live among thieves and infamous folk, that our conversation might be virtuous and our ways right ways.

That suffering of theirs has, perhaps, been rewarded by the vision of the ease they won for us. Their spirits may be moving about us, touching us, rejoicing that evil days should have purchased happy days, and well content that misery should have brought such treasure. Let us hope so, at anyrate. Let us think, too, that patriotism, in its true form, is of the kind they gave. It is not a song in the street, and a wreath on a column, and a flag flying from a window, and a pro-Boer under a pump. It is a thing very holy, and very terrible, like life itself. It is a burden to be borne; a thing to labour for and to suffer for and to die for; a thing which gives no happiness and no pleasantness—but a hard life, an unknown grave, and the respect and bared heads of those who follow.

BIBLIOGRAPHY

This book is necessarily condensed. It indicates, very briefly, some of the aspects of sea life in the Royal Navy during the latter years of Nelson's career. Any reader desiring to learn more of that way of life will find the following authorities of service to him; they are some of the books from which the present writer has extracted his information:—

Admiralty Regulations and Instructions, 1734
Admiralty Regulations and Instructions, 1766
Admiralty Regulations and Instructions, 1790
Admiralty Regulations and Instructions, 1808
Admiralty Regulations for the Exercise of Great Guns in H.M. Ships, 1764

Barker, M.H.	*Greenwich Hospital*
Barker, M.H.	*The "Victory"*
Barker, M.H.	*The Naval Club*
Blane, J.	*Diseases of Seamen, 1785*
Brenton, E.P.	*Life of Earl St Vincent*
Broadhead, A.G.	*The Navy as It is*
Captain in the Navy	*Observations*
Charnock, W.	*Marine Architecture*
Clowes, Sir W. Laird	*History of the Royal Navy*
Cochrane, T.	*Autobiography*
Cochrane, T.	*Observations on Naval Affairs*
Coke, Hon. Henry	*Tracks of a Rolling Stone*
Collingwood, G.L.N.	*Life and Letters of Lord Collingwood*
Congreve, Sir W.	*The Mounting of Naval Ordnance*
Davis, Joshua	*Narrative*
Derrick, C.	*Memoirs of the Royal Navy*
Douglas, Sir. H.	*Naval Gunnery*
Dundas, Lord	*A Fair Statement*
Edye, L.	*Records of the Royal Marines*
Falconer, R.	*Dictionary of the Marine, 1789*
Falconer, R.	*Dictionary of the Marine, Burney's edition, 1815*
Glascock, W.N.	*Naval Service*
Glascock, W.N.	*Naval Sketch Book*
Glascock, W.N.	*Tales of a Tar*
Glascock, W.N.	*The Night Watch*
Glascock, W.N.	*Land Sharks and Sea Gulls*
Greener, W.	*The Gun*
Griffiths, A.L.	*Observations on Seamanship*
Hall, B., Capt.	*The Midshipman*
Hall, B., Capt.	*The Lieutenant and Commander*
Hamilton, Sir E.	*Story of the "Hermione."*

James, W..	*Naval History*	
Leech, Samuel	*Thirty Years from Home*	
Leslie, R.C.	*Old Sea Wings, Ways, and Words*	
Liddel, R.	*Seaman's Vade Mecum*	
Lind, J.	*Essay on the Health of Seamen*	
Long, W.H.	*Naval Yarns*	
Marks, E.C.R.	*Evolution of Modern Small Arms*	
Marryat, F.	*Impressment in the Royal Navy*	
Maydman, H.	*Naval Speculations*	
Melville, Herman . . .	*White Jacket*	
Miles, E.	*Epitome of the Royal Navy*	
Mitford, Jack	*Johnny Newcome in the Navy*	
Moyle, Jasper	*Chirurgus Marinus*	
Nasty-Face, Jack . . .	*Nautical Economy*	
Naval Chronicle, 1799-1805 .		
Naval Exhibition Catalogue, 1891		
Naval Orders and Statutes		
Navy at Home, The		
Neale, W.J.	*History of the Mutiny at Spithead*	
O'Brien, D.H. . . .	*My Adventures*	
Officer in Royal Navy . .	*An Address, 1787*	
Old Naval Surgeon . . .	*An Address to Officers*	
Old Seaman	*Impressment*	
Orders in Council for H.M. Navy		
Ricketts, Captain . . .	*Popularity of the Royal Navy*	
Robinson, Commander C.N. .	*The British Fleet*	
Schomberg, J.	*Naval Chronology*	
Scott, Michael	*Cruise of the "Midge"*	
Sinclair, A.	*Reminiscences*	
Smollett, T.	*Works, edition 1797*	
Somerville, A.	*Autobiography*	
Statutes Relating to H.M. Navy		
Steel, T.	*Seamanship*	
Thompson, E.	*Sailor's Letters*	
Urquhart, T.	*Evils of Impressment*	
Ward, E.	*Wooden World dissected*	

To this list may be added the nautical novels of Captains Marryat and Chamier; a number of manuscripts in the British Museum and Public Record Office; the works of Garneray and De la Graviere; one or two obscure books of seamanship, and articles in *Blackwood, The Nautical Magazine, The English Historical Review, The Fortnightly,* and other reviews. I have also consulted the models at Greenwich, the Trinity House, and the United Service Institution, and the nautical prints at the British Museum.

INDEX

Able whackets, 37
Admiral, 24, (n) 98
Admiralty flag, 98
After-guard, 58
Animals, 78
Apron, 16
Assistant surgeon, 43

Battle lanterns, 11
Beer, 30,67
Berths, 61, 62
Bluejacket, 55
Boarders, 22
Boarding-axe, 22
Boarding-pike, 22
Boatswain, 44 *et seq.*
Boatswain's mate, 45
Booms, 8
Bore, 14
Boys, ship's 54
Brass guns, 14
Bread-room, 13
Breech, 14
Breechings, 15
Bull's-eyes, 11
Bullying, 38

Cabins, 8, 12
Cable, 12
Cable tiers, 12
Cannon, 14 *et seq.*
Captain, duties, etc.,
    51 *et seq.*
Captain's fancies, 28
Captain's powers, 26 *et seq.*
Captain's uniform, 28
Carpenter, 50 *et seq.*
Carriages, gun, 14,15
Carronades, 14,20
Cartridges, 13, 16

Cascabel, 14
Cat. *See* punishment, 71
Chaplain, 43, 44
Chesapeake, 83
Cleaning decks, 85,87,88
Clearing for action, 77
Cobbing, 37
Cockpits, 12, 41 *et seq.*
Collingwood, 72
Commodore, 24
Cook, ship's, 52
Cook, mess 66
Copper-sheathing, 2
Corporals, ship's, 52
Cross-jack, 4,8
Cutlasses, 22

Decks, 10,11,12
Decks, in action, 80 *et seq.*
Disinfection, 39, 40 *et seq.*
Divine service, 88
Drunkenness, 68,72,89,
    92,93

Entry port, 7
Epilogue, 100
Establishment, the, 3,4

Figurehead, 6
Fish-room, 13
Flags, 98,99
Flint-locks, 17
Flogging. *See* punishment
    27
Forecastle, 8,9
Forecastle men, 57
Fumigations, 40,41
    et seq.

Galley, 10

Gangways, 8
Gingerbread work, 9
Glims, 12
Grog, 68,73,87,89
Gunner, 49 *et seq.*
Guns, 14,15,20,78 *et seq.*
    long and short, 18,19,20
Gun-room, 11
Grampussing, 37

Halberds, 22
Half-deck, 9
Half-ports, 23
Hammocks, 59,62,77,
    85,87
Hammock cloths, 77
Hammock nettings, 8
Handspike, 18
Hermione, H.M.S., 97
Hold, 13

Idlers, 59,84

Jews, 91

Keel, 1
Keel, false, 1
Kit, 62

Ladle, 16
Leaks, 11
Lifebuoys, 8
Light-rooms, 13
Linstock, 17
Lower-deck, etc., 13
Lord Mayor's men, 25, 39
Lieutenant, duties, etc., 28
Lieutenant, powers, 28
Lieutenant, uniform, 30

Magazines, 13
Main-deck, 10
Manger, 11
Manning, 24 *et seq.*
Marines, 69, 78
Marine Society, 54
Marryat, Captain, 25,27
Master, 30,31
Master's duties, 31
Master's uniform, 31
Master's mates, 31,32
Master-at-arms, 51,72,81,
     86,87,92
Masts, 3, 4
Mast-heading, 36
Mast-pond, 3
Match, 17
Meals, 60
Messes, 60
Midshipmen, 11,32
     et seq. 86
Midshipmen's berth, 34
     et seq.
Misfire, 18
Mould-lofts, 1
Muskets, 21
Musketoon, 22
Muster book, 25
Mutinies, 97,98

Nastyface, Jack, 74
Nelson, 72
Nelson chequer, 6
Nore, mutiny at the,
     97, 98

Oak, 1
Oak, American, 2
Oldsters, 33
Orlop, 12 *et seq.* 39

Parker, Sir Peter, 38
Painting, external, 6

Painting, internal, 7
Painting masts, etc., 7
Pendants, 98
Pigtails, 63
Piping the side, 27
Pistols, 22
Pomelion, 15
Poop, 7.8.9
Ports, 22
Port-riggles, 23
Port-tackles, 22
Press-gangs, 24, 25, 55
Pressed men, 24
Priming, 16
Priming-iron, 16
Priming-tube, 16
Provisions, 64
Purser, 47 *et seq.*
Punishments, 58,71, *et seq.*

Quarter-deck, 7.8.9
Quarter-gallery, 6,9
Quartermaster, 51
Quotamen, 56

Rammer, 18
Ranges, 19,21
Rates, 5
Recoil, 17,18
Rigging, 3,4

Sailmaker, 51
Sail-room, 12
Salutes, 98
Schoolmaster, 44
Screen, 13
Sheathing, 2
Ships, 1,4,5
Ships, French and Spanish,
     4,5
Ships, unrated, 5
Shot, 20 *et seq.*
Shot, varieties, 21

Shot-racks, 12
Sick-bay, 39,41
Side-ropes, 7
Side-tackles, 15
Slops, 47 *et seq.*
Small-arms, 21
Smoking, 51
Songs, 94,95,96
Spirit-room, 13
Spithead, mutiny at, 97,98
Splinters, 21
Sponge, 18
St George's banner, 98
State-rooms, 10
Steerage, 9
Stern-light, 8
Stern-walks, 6
Stern-works, 6

Tackles (side) 15
Tackles (train), 15
Thieving. *See* punishment.
Tiller ropes, 8
Timbers, 2
Tompion, 15
Topmen, 57
Touch-hole, 16
Tree-nails, 2
Tripping, 15
Turn out, 37

Ulcers, 39

Wads, 16
Waist, 8, 81
Waisters, 58
Watch, 84,87
Water-casks, 30
Wives, 92, etc.
Women, 92
Worm, 18

Youngsters, 32

A Selected List of Books Published by
CONWAY MARITIME PRESS LIMITED
Details of forthcoming books will be sent post free on request :—

A NARRATIVE OF THE BATTLE OF ST. VINCENT
With Anecdotes of Nelson Before and After the Battle
by Col. Drinkwater Bethune.
An Eye Witness Account of this celebrated action
Reprint of 1840 edition
112 pages 9 battle plans. ISBN 0 85177 000 2   £1.50

A BIBLIOGRAPHY OF BRITISH NAVAL HISTORY
A biographical and historical guide to printed and historical sources.
by G.E. Manwaring
163 pages. ISBN 0 85177 006 1   £3.50

A MARINER OF ENGLAND
An account of the career of William Richardson from cabin boy in the merchant service to Warrant Officer in the Royal Navy 1780—1819 as told by himself.
by Col. Spencer Childers (Ed.)
336 pages. Frontis. ISBN 0 85177 015 0   £2.50

FAMOUS FRIGATE ACTIONS
The hard fought duels of frigates, corvettes, sloops-of-war and brigs
by C.R. Low
256 pages. 8 plates ISBN 0 85177 008 8   £3.00

THE OLD EAST INDIAMEN
The story of the most amazingly powerful trading concern which the world has ever known and in particular the men and the ships of this golden age.
by E. Keble Chatterton
308 pages. 15 illustrations. ISBN 0 85177 016 9   £3.25

FIGHTING INSTRUCTIONS 1530—1816
The art of naval tactics and its history.
by Sir Julian S. Corbett
382 pages. ISBN 0 85177 039 8   £4.75

SIGNALS AND INSTRUCTIONS 1776—1794
Sailing Tactics based upon the Bridport Papers, the Rodney Papers and the collection of Admiral Sir Thomas Graves, K.B.
by Sir Julian S. Corbett
403 pages. ISBN 0 85177 038 X   £4.75

MODERN HISTORY OF WARSHIPS
"Not dated despite its age. All types of warships in all the navies of any consequence in the iron-clad age; also chapters on design and construction of hull, machinery, ordnance, mines and torpedoes, and protection. The author was Professor of Naval Design and Construction Massachusetts Institute of Technology. *A.J. Marder. From the Dreadnought to Scapa Flow Vol. V.*"
by William Hovgaard. With a new Introduction by Antony M. Preston.
502 pages. 209 illustrations. 6 folding plans. ISBN 0 85177 040 1   £8.50

THE SEAMAN'S VADE MECUM, and Defensive War by Sea. 1756
Detailed Information about the equipment, drills and routine relating to ships of the Royal Navy and dealing also with merchant ship practice.
by William Mountaine F.R.S.
Leather. Slip Case. ISBN 0 85177 037 1   £7.00

INDEX TO JAMES NAVAL HISTORY
In four parts:— British and Foreign Ships, Naval Officers, Military Officers and Naval Actions.
by C.G. Toogood. Edited by R.A. Brassey.
Reprint of 1895 Edition
188 pages. ISBN 0 85177 017 7   £3.00

THE HUDSON'S BAY COMPANY Its Position and Prospects
The substance of an address to a meeting of the shareholders in January, 1866
by James Dodds
80 pages with folding maps. ISBN 0 85177 001 0   £1.25

OLD WHALING DAYS
Arctic Whaling during the Last Years of the Sailing Whaler.
by Captain William Barron.
Reprint of 1895 edition.
211 pages. Maps and Plates. ISBN 0 85177 007 X   £3.00

LIFE ABOARD A BRITISH PRIVATEER
The Journal of Captain Woodes Rogers' voyage round the world in the ships "Duke" and "Dutchess" 1708—1711
by R.C. Leslie (Ed.)
143 pages. Plates. ISBN 0 85177 009 6   £2.50

A TREATISE ON NAVAL ARCHITECTURE
Founded upon Philosophical and Rational Principles towards establishing fixed rules for the best form and proportional dimensions in Length, Breadth and Depth of Merchant Ships in general and also the Management of them to the greatest advantage by Practical Seamanship; with important remarks relating thereto especially both for Defence and Attacks in War at Sea, from long approved experience.
by William Hutchinson – Mariner, 1794. – New Imp. 1971.
303 pages. Frontis & 12 plates. ISBN 0 85177 002 9   £6.00

AT WAR WITH THE SMUGGLERS
The career of Dr. Arnold's father, Collector of Customs in the Isle of Wight, from 1777.
by D. Arnold Forster.
New impression 1971 of 1936 Edition.
256 pages. Illustrated. ISBN 0 85177 011 8   £2.50

THE LAST OF A GLORIOUS ERA
The last and most famous days of the sailing ship.
by Ronald Pearse.
Illustrated with 79 contemporary photographs.
New impression 1969. ISBN 0 85177 000 2   £2.25

WAR AT SEA Modern Theory and Ancient Practice
by Admiral Sir Reginald Custance
113 pages. 12 plans and charts. New impression 1970. ISBN 0 85177 012 6   £2.50

SAILING BARGES
by F.G.G. Carr
New Impression 1971 of the Revised 1951 Edition
350 pages. Over 100 Illustrations. ISBN 0 85177 024 X   £4.20

COLLIER BRIGS AND THEIR SAILORS
by Sir Walter Runciman Bt., with an introduction by Basil Greenhill.
First published 1926, New Impression 1971.
288 pages. 23 illustrations. ISBN 0 85177 043 6   £3.80

THE MAGIC OF THE SWATCHWAYS
by Maurice Griffiths, G.M.
New Impression 1971 of 1951 edition.
235 pages. 7 illustrations. ISBN 0 85177 045 2   £2.80

THE FIRST RAILWAY IN LONDON
The Story of the London and Greenwich Railway from 1832–1878
by Alfred Rosling Bennet, M.I.E.E.
48 pages. 45 Illustrations. ISBN 0 85177 046 0
New Impression 1971 of 1912 Edition   £1.80

OUT OF APPLEDORE
The Autobiography of a coastal shipmaster and shipowner in the last days of wooden sailing ships.
by W.J. Slade. Edited and with a new Introduction by Basil Greenhill.
New Impression 1971 of 1959 Edition.
124 pages. 20 Plates ISBN 0 85177 026 6   £2.00

GREENWICH PARK   Its History and Associations
by A.D. Webster. Superintendent of Greenwich Park.
New Impression 1971 of 1902 Edition.
103 pages. 31 illustrations. ISBN 0 85177 036 3   £2.00

HISTORY OF LEE AND ITS NEIGHBOURHOOD
by F.H. Hart
New Impression 1971 of 1882 Edition
112 pages. Frontis. ISBN 0 85177 035 5   £1.75

THE HISTORY OF DEPTFORD
by Nathan Dews
New Impression 1971 of 1884 Revised Edition.
328 pages. Map and Illustrations. ISBN 0 85177 041 X   £2.50

BRITISH WARSHIPS OF THE SECOND WORLD WAR
A Folio of authentic scale plans of: *Rodney, Royal Oak, Warspite, Renown, Repulse, Ajax London, Manchester, Sussex, Ariadne, Onslow, Lance.*
by Alan Ravan and John Roberts.
Each Plan measures 14½″ x 30½″ folding to 14½″ x 10½″. The Plans are extremely accurate and detailed and a short history accompanies each ship. ISBN 0 85177 021 5   £2.80

CONWAY MARITIME PRESS LIMITED
7 Nelson Road, Greenwich, London, S.E.10
Tel: 01-858 7211